Ed Wynn's Son

Ed Wynn's Son

by

KEENAN WYNN

as told to

JAMES BROUGH

Garden City, New York

DOUBLEDAY & COMPANY, INC.

1959

Library of Congress Catalog Card Number 59-12663

Copyright © 1959 by Keenan Wynn and James Brough

Copyright © 1959 by McCall Corporation

All Rights Reserved

Printed in the United States of America

The only Man that e're I knew
Who did not make me almost spew
Was Fuseli: He was both Turk and Jew—
And so, dear Christian Friends, how do you do?

—WILLIAM BLAKE

This is the story of my father, Ed Wynn, and myself, and the troubles that grew between us. Some things in this book may seem strange to many people, but I have tried, as honestly as possible, to relate what happened to us and what I thought about it *at the time*.

I emphasize *at the time*, because today of course my opinions have changed about events that took place twenty and thirty years ago. I used to think sometimes that I was a poor little rich boy and feel very sorry for myself. I used to be afraid that I never would get out from under Dad's shadow, and I resented it bitterly. But all that is in the past.

The special things that happened to me caused us both a lot of unhappiness. To a great extent, they contributed to what I made of myself, but the important thought here is that a man can make himself what he is, not let outside forces shape his life completely.

I believe that every son—and daughter—faces problems in growing up. If the father happens to be forceful or famous—and Dad was both—then those problems become more acute. But nobody can afford to let self-pity ruin his life. This I've learned.

I have also learned to be myself, an entity, doing as well as I can as an actor and a human being. I am still extremely conscious of being Ed Wynn's son, but . . . Well, this is the story.

K.W.

Part One

I woke up thinking about John Wilkes Booth again. I used to feel a grisly kind of sympathy for him when I began as an actor myself, a half-savage, semiliterate kid who knew about girls, and fast boats, and not much else. I thought we had something in common; he was an actor's son with problems too.

I used to read in the dressing rooms about him and his father, Junius Brutus Booth, the first great actor in America and a philosophical drunk who overshadowed his son. When John Booth played his first stage parts, the critics of his day thought he had real talent, more in some ways than his elder brother Edwin.

He used to play to packed houses in New York and Philadelphia. In Boston, at the old Museum Theatre, he was the greatest hit of his time, and women used to crowd around the stage doors to admire him. In the theatrical sense he was a good actor, but when he assassinated Lincoln he was of course rated a very bad actor indeed.

Yet good or bad (I was thinking) John Wilkes Booth was the only actor the whole world remembered. In my profession the great old names were usually forgotten. Kean, Garrick, Sheridan—who gave a damn about any of them?

Irving, Cohan, John Barrymore—nobody spared them a thought except a few old-timers in The Players.

It seemed like a sad state of affairs to me. Here was John Booth, who murdered a president and was remembered. There was Edwin Booth, who was forgotten. It apparently made no difference how good or bad an actor you were, you hadn't a hope of surviving unless you did something other than acting.

I couldn't think of any member of my profession who was remembered in history except for one thing, and that was scandal. You could start anywhere in the past to prove that point. The favorites of the day were forgotten in a year or so unless scandal was somehow linked with their names.

Nell Gwyn, fascinating and profane, didn't owe her reputation to performances in any theatre. Fatty Arbuckle's name lingered, not because he was a good comedian, but because he was convicted of doing something scandalous to a girl.

Public regard for people like me was a passing fancy. Take the greatest living actor, Sir Laurence Olivier. Take a powerful American actor like Marlon Brando. Our reputations, if any, would die with us—and probably long before that—unless we achieved something else. We were all basically unimportant people. Without a conviction for rape or murder, we were all going to be forgotten in the wink of an eye.

On July 27, 1959, I reached the age of forty-three, having appeared in 107 Equity plays of various descriptions and more than 90 movies. Chances were I'd passed the halfway mark of my life, yet here I was, working in a completely unimportant business, trying to be some sort of artist in an art form of little consequence. From the time I climbed out of bed, it turned out to be a day for brooding.

"I think," I said at dinner, "that I should have done something else with my time."

"Like what?" said Sharley, who is my wife.

"I don't know. I don't see myself doing anything else. I've no training except for the job I'm in."

"Well, you ran that car agency with Tom Bamford."

"That was more of a hobby," I said.

"Anyway, you'd miss the excitement and everything."

"Honey, that's all bull. There's this wonderful thing about actors. Heroic and exciting as they try to be, they really don't amount to much."

Sharley, who is twenty-five, has a straightforward mind. She put down her fork and said, "What about everything you've earned in your business? Not just the money, but other things. You know, fame and a kind of power. All that."

"Bull. Take money. We've always eaten, sure. But our daughters are being brought up on far less money than Dad made. And my sons don't live with us."

"Okay then. What about the fame?"

"Bull again. Who wants it? If you care about it, there's only one advantage to fame, and that's been well said by that wonderful woman, Marlene Dietrich. She once said to me, 'It's worth all the trouble so long as the service is good.'"

Sharley was getting restless. "There's power then."

"That's ridiculous. Maybe it's great for just a few, and they like to feel they can make people behave. But that's not for me. An actor with a power complex is usually a horse's laugh. Most of us are lucky if we've got enough power to pick up a pay check."

She reached for a cigarette, and her eyes flashed. "You make me mad sometimes, you honestly do. Look at everything you've achieved. You ought to take some pride in that."

I stopped to think. I tried to make a list of achievements in my head, forgetting nothing, for Sharley's sake. I wanted to be fair in this argument.

I had achieved, as the result of a somewhat unpleasant

accident, a silver plug embedded by surgeons in my skull, which my friend Jim Backus christened my "silver tea service for four."

I had retained a nodding acquaintance with the abilities of internal-combustion engines, whether in sports cars, aircraft, motorcycles, or powerboats.

Creating an acting role was something I could do without too much trouble; acting, in fact, was probably a little too easy for the good of my soul.

I'd made friendships with a gratifying number of people, including two men—Hector Alexander and Cary Loftin—whom I'd trust to the death. I'd also managed to keep the friendship of my first wife, Evie, and my good friend whom she married, Van Johnson.

I had achieved two sons and two daughters by way of three wives, to one of whom I am most satisfactorily married.

I was credited in some circles with having lizard blood because of the speed with which I recovered from assorted hurts and broken bones suffered in the pursuit of pleasure over the past twenty-seven years.

And that just about covered it. At forty-three, it seemed I hadn't discovered yet where I was going. The reasons weren't hard to find. You could trace them back to an upbringing best described as irregular.

God knows, I thought, I've no patience with the self-pity that swallows most of my contemporaries in similar situations. But it was very clear to me that I had grown up both early and late. Without going through the psychoanalysis rigmarole, I realized I grew up late, in wanting to prove courage and rebellion in racing cars and motor bikes beyond an age where most men settle for gentler pastimes. But as a kid I grew up in an emotional hurry, of necessity, because I was confronted with situations no schoolboy has the mental equipment to handle. I was simultaneously both young and old.

For this I used always to blame my father, Ed Wynn.

I picked up the telephone and dialed his number. I could hear the ringing in his apartment and picture him walking across his living room. After we'd said hello, I got to what I had in mind: "Pop, I'm going to write a book."

There was a pause at the other end. "A book about what, Keenan?"

"About us. The family. What we've done."

He turned the idea over for a moment. "Will there be some laughs?"

"Some," I said. "It won't be like 'Let's lie down on a couch with a typewriter.' But we weren't exactly funny people all the time."

I could feel the old tenseness that used to come even when I heard Dad's name. For most of my life I resented him beyond reason.

"If you do a book," he was saying, "don't forget your fourth birthday. We had a wonderful party."

"I won't," I promised. I remembered the days when I was happy to be Ed Wynn's son. Then there were years when I could scarcely bring myself to speak to him. The bitterness was fading fast. What remained was the tenseness, the uncomfortable feeling of a man recovering from surgery before the stitches are taken out.

He had two more things to say before we said good night: "Don't make me the heavy."

"It wasn't that simple."

And: "You can't tell the whole truth, Keenan."

"Maybe not," I said, "but I can try."

II

Truth has been notoriously elusive since the day of Pontius Pilate. From my viewpoint, the most important event in my family happened one May morning four years before I was born. In a drafty corridor of the Orpheum Theatre, Winnipeg, Dad met the girl who became my mother. Her name was Hilda Keenan, and she was beautiful. They had arrived at the stage door by their separate ways to open the following day.

At the age of twenty-six, Dad topped the bill with an English comic, Edmond Russon, in a sketch called *Joy and Gloom.* On the billboards outside the biggest type announced the extra, added attraction: "Frank Keenan and His Company in Oliver White's Intense Playlet, *Man to Man.*" Hilda Keenan appeared with her father.

In her high-laced walking boots and long hobble skirt, this eighteen-year-old girl looked like an Irish countess, black Irish maybe, with dark hair and piercing blue eyes. Dad was a thin young man with glasses, a long, bony face. He was enormously impressed. He remembered later: "She was the cutest thing in girls I ever saw."

This was 1912. My mother and father had no way of knowing the pain the future held when they first stopped to say hello. They must have talked about the weather—spring arrives cold and late that far north—and the *Titanic*, which had sunk a few weeks earlier. When my grandfather came on the scene, they inevitably talked politics, since he was a lifelong Democrat; Bryan and Al Smith were his idols.

Frank Keenan didn't think much of the giggling, determined young man who was billed as "The Boy with the Funny Hat." Dad was earning three hundred dollars a week, which was big money in pre-war vaudeville, but my grandfather had a lordly disregard for such things. "I have lived as well as any millionaire," he used to say without exaggeration.

Dad had already made his Broadway debut four years previously in *The Deacon and the Lady*, but he hadn't moved up to star status yet. At fifty-four, my grandfather was a great name in the theatre, commanding both physically and intellectually; six feet three inches tall, with a mind like a lash. He was a star in movies along with Clara Kimball Young, Milton Sills, and Alice Brady. Who remembers him now? Outside of my family, only Ethel Barrymore used to mention his name when we met.

He was that rarity in the theater of his day, a college man —Boston College—but he never graduated. He commissioned plays for himself. He once commanded the playwright George Creel, "Go down to the park and sit on a bench for half an hour. I'll lay you whatever you want to bet that there will be more moving tragedy and more human comedy on that bench than anything you've written or anything you could write out of your imagination alone."

He pre-dated Stanislavski. "I read everything I can find on the period," he once explained, "the characters, the performances of other actors, and I make notes as I read. Then I assemble and build up the character." That's how he set about creating the star role of a city editor in a drama called

Todd of the Times. He reasoned that a newspaperman worked grueling hours, bolted his meals, hurried back to a desk full of telephones. So on that desk Frank Keenan put the prop that explained the character: a can of bicarbonate of soda.

My mother admired, defied, and despaired of her father all at the same time, in a mixture of Irish emotions. She'd had no ambition except to be an actress and appear with him, and she promised to be an exceedingly good actress. With her sister Frances, my aunt whom we called Fuff, she practiced hard at piano and singing so that she could meet his exacting standards.

An actor's life was spent either in furnished apartments or leather trunks and wicker baskets. You played one year on Broadway—when you signed a lease on your apartment—before you took the play on tour for twelve months, with your belongings riding in the baggage car. This was the true family theatre. It nourished the long line of Drews, Booths, and Barrymores, and three generations of Keenans, including myself.

It was hard to tell which Keenan impressed my dad the more: the father with the astrakhan-collared topcoat or the daughter with the sparkling eyes. He made up his mind to marry the daughter and model himself on her majestic parent. There was one thing about Frank Keenan, however, that he didn't suspect, an extra added reason why his daughter traveled with him. Besides playing a doctor's secretary in *Man to Man,* she was a nurse to her father. Frank Keenan was a monumental drunk.

In theatrical terms he was a "furniture actor," and not alone in that category. With a bottle of liquor in him, he could still breeze impressively through a performance, so long as he had a piece of furniture to clutch with one hand and another actor to cling to if he had to make any move around the stage. But he had to stay on his feet. If he sat down, nobody could get him on his legs again while the curtain was up.

But I imagine my dad had a kind of hero worship for Frank Keenan. Here was a man he suspected he never could be, a theatrical aristocrat where my father was a clown. He did his best to look like his future father-in-law. He wore the same style of gray fedora and tight-buttoned suits. He sported a similar cane, wore a similar flower in his lapel. One of the few things he didn't copy were my grandfather's pince-nez, worn on a grosgrain cord that dangled around his neck.

Frank Keenan was never one of Dad's fans in those days; that came later. A two-man comedy act like Wynn and Russon was not dignified entertainment, and Frank Keenan was as dignified as a renegade priest. He still thought of comedians as red-nosed clowns swatting each other with pigs' bladders and chasing each other around the stage as an encore. Dad used to explain proudly, "We stand still and cut out the swatting." Frank Keenan remained unimpressed.

Dad's act was the same in style and spirit as the one he'd put together nine years earlier when he wandered around New York trying to get himself hired. He knew unknown kids didn't stand a chance with the bookers. He needed strategy, and he got an idea.

Back home in Philadelphia, he had watched an act called Murray and Mack. He discovered that in New York they also ran a booking agency in a building at Thirty-ninth Street and Broadway. He realized he'd have to make an impression on them somehow, so he invented one of his first bits of business. He would open the door of their outer office, start to say, "Well, I just dropped in to see you," and then fall flat on his face. The sight of him stretched on the floor would bring Murray and Mack running. Then he'd sit up and break into his best, quick-fire monologue. They wouldn't be able to resist him, and he'd pick up a job. That, anyway, was the way he daydreamed it.

He circled the block for an hour, getting up his courage. He climbed the stairs to the office, flung open the door, gabbled his line, and took a full-length fall, exactly as planned. But, lying on the linoleum, he couldn't hear a sound. He blinked one eye open, then sat up in a hurry. The office was deserted. The staff, including Murray and Mack, had gone out to lunch.

Dad arrived in New York in April 1902 with his mind set on being a comic. He dropped in by chance at a rathskeller on West Forty-third Street run by Kid McCoy, who had retired from the prize ring to go into the restaurant business. At the bar downstairs Dad met two young men, George Whiting and Jack Lewis, who were keeping the customers entertained by singing and playing the piano.

Dad said later, "Lewis took me for a rich man's son who would make good pickings. I told him I was an actor looking for a partner. We joined up, and he lived off me for weeks, with neither of us working. My dear mother was very thoughtful, so we never wanted for money."

They were two of a kind, brash kids, hungry to be famous. They got up a double act they called *The Rah! Rah! Boys,* in which Dad played a college freshman and Jack Lewis a sophomore, two dudes with patent-leather hair and deckchair striped blazers. No booker would look at them.

Then that summer Dad heard a benefit variety show was going to be staged at the West End Theatre up on 125th Street for a man called Sugarman. The headliner and master of ceremonies was to be Jim Corbett, the former world heavyweight champion, whom Lewis knew as an occasional customer at Kid McCoy's. Wynn and Lewis decided to crash the stage door.

Their props, when they arrived, included a skullcap, walk-

ing cane, cap pistol, and waddling bulldog. The doorman
would not let them in. "I'm Jim Corbett's cousin from out
West," said Lewis, which got them inside.

Corbett agreed to let them go on. "It's a tough crowd,"
he warned them. "You'd better be good or they'll bounce
you on the sidewalk."

He introduced them as "a celebrated comedy act from
California." Out from the wings skipped the two dudes singing, "Rah, rah, rah! Who pays my bills? Ma and Pa!" Jack
somehow managed to twirl the cane, smoke a meerschaum
pipe, and keep hold of the bulldog. Dad wore the skullcap,
waved the cap gun, and punctuated the patter with the
repeated cry of "Grape-Nuts!"

The audience went for it in a big way. In the orchestra
seats sat a vaudeville booker, Joe Shea. As soon as the curtain
went down on *The Rah! Rah! Boys,* he went backstage. Would
they take two hundred dollars a week to open the following
day at the Colonial, which was the top spot in vaudeville
at that time? They grabbed at the chance, repeated their
success, and toured their act for the next two years.

"I had an attack of the biggest head you ever saw," Dad
remembered later. "How could it be otherwise? From being
absolutely unknown and out of work to getting on at the
Colonial, all in no time at all, would turn anyone's head,
much less the heads of a couple of boys."

Dad's early acts were as remote from Frank Keenan's way
of earning a living as anything could be. But at the end of
the run in Winnipeg, when *Man to Man* and *Joy and Gloom*
gypsied on to new bookings in other towns, Hilda Keenan
and Ed Wynn kept in close touch. On September 4, 1914,
they were married.

My mother married for love. I think, too, she was swept
up by Dad's drive toward success. The excitement of it was
infectious. He certainly married for the same reason, though

love was a complex emotion for him. In the first years of marriage he idolized her beyond any human ability to live up to the image.

My father lived in a dream world of his own creating, in which the reality was his will to succeed. It was a world as quaint as a nursery tale, where the babies came out of cabbages, toilets didn't exist, and there was nothing as disturbing as passion or prejudice. Nobody ever got a bellyache, only a "stomach distress."

"To tell the truth, Keenan," he has said, "I never wanted to be a real person."

Husband and wife were totally different people in natures and upbringing. My mother was an emotional Irish girl, whose family cherished the legend that they were descended from Irish kings. She had been brought up as a worldly young sophisticate, had toured with her sister in an act of their own, playing two grand pianos and singing duets.

The Keenans were stanch Catholics. My mother had been educated by nuns, and she clung to her religion with a frightening intensity. My grandfather held similar fierce beliefs. He was too urbane to echo openly the intolerance of some fellow Catholics, but it colored his thinking. Preoccupation with questions of race. Prejudice dating back to Christ on the Cross. He had been dead set against his daughter's marriage. Because she was strong-minded enough to enjoy defying her father, that gave her an additional reason for going through with it in a civil ceremony.

She ignored the words her father once used in his vain attempts to prevent the wedding: "Why the devil do you want to marry a Jew?" For six months afterward, he shut his daughter and son-in-law out of his life.

Then chance put Frank Keenan and Ed Wynn on the same bill in Chicago and into the same hotel, the Sherman House. My grandfather found himself in the same elevator with them and promptly turned his back. When my mother started to cry, Dad tackled him.

"This is silly, you know," he said. "I'm your son-in-law, and nothing can change that."

Grandpa Keenan looked down at him and began to chuckle. Dad smiled too, and my mother dried her tears. "I guess it is a good idea at that," my grandfather said, "to have a Jew up your sleeve."

III

My father was born Isaiah Edwin Leopold. Grandpa and Grandma Leopold had a hard time breaking themselves of the habit of calling him Iz. He had an older brother, Leon, and he began cutting capers in the first place as a typical younger child trying to get attention.

The first props he used were the women's hats Grandpa Joseph Leopold manufactured in the business he owned at 702 Arch Street in Philadelphia. My grandfather also owned several unambitious shops that sold women's millinery.

He was a Bohemian Jew who believed he had discarded much of his European Jewishness, and there was little evidence of Jewry in his cozy house on Kensington Avenue. My grandmother was born in Turkey of a family of Sephardic Jews. She had a dark olive skin that contrasted startlingly with her bright blue eyes. She landed as an immigrant with her family when she was four years old. I remember her elegant hats, tall boots, and how she had to walk leaning on the arm of her companion, "Aunt" Lizzie. A birth deformity had been botched by surgeons who tried to correct it when she was eighteen, and she was consequently crippled.

Little Minnie Leopold kept up some of the ways her parents had brought with them, though to gentile eyes she was the least Jewish-looking member of the family. I can still remember the familiar odors of her cooking—chicken soup with noodles, meat balls and rice cooked in cabbage leaves, milk-sauce fish, and the other delicacies that intrigued me when I visited my grandparents.

My grandfather Leopold regarded himself as a strictly American businessman to whom rabbinical law meant less than his office ledgers. Dad set great store by one of his father's maxims: "Never worry about anything money can buy."

The Leopolds were a solid middle-class family; they first realized their younger son was something different when he was seven years old, according to one of my dad's stories. His father had bought four tickets to a show that was playing that week at the Walnut Street Theatre, the oldest continuing theatre in the United States, dating back to the 1800s. They would all leave home soon after dinner, he explained to Iz, because the curtain would go up at eight o'clock. In mid-afternoon Iz began crying, and none of them could stop his tears. Why? "I want eight o'clock to be *now*," he sobbed.

He got home that night, talking about being a comedian. His father scorned the idea. "You've got to amount to something. Finish school, graduate from college, then come into millinery with me."

Relatives—there were dozens within visiting distance—were brought in to persuade Iz that his father was right. But Iz could keep the relatives laughing and convulse the salesgirls when he called at one of the shops and tried on the stock. Iz, in a cartwheel hat dressed up like a Schrafft's fruit salad, was a sight to see.

The Leopolds used to spend their summers in Atlantic City, where sun, sand, and idle spectators always drove Iz to outdo himself. In a knee-length wool bathing suit, he'd do anything for a laugh, including leaping from the

Steel Pier clutching one of his father's headpieces. After a season or so he was called "the clown of the beach."

At that time I don't think he had caught as much as a whiff of anti-Semitism. As a boy, he used to imagine he was a Moslem with a Rumanian father. Philadelphia was spared the ghetto living that blighted nineteenth-century Chicago and other cities. Jews were comparatively well accepted along Chestnut Street and in some suburbs. The men who owned and worked in millinery and tailoring made up a city within a city and mixed mostly with fellow Hebrews. Within those limits, the Leopolds lived securely in a sort of self-made sanctuary. Iz was not aware of his race especially until he met Hilda Keenan.

He was cajoled by his father to enter high school, but he'd no time to waste on an education. When the Balbazoo Club, which was a local amateur theatrical society, accepted him for membership at fifteen, his enthusiasm for clowning took a sharp upward turn. He signed his father's name to an excuse from school "to see the doctor." Instead, he scurried into a vaudeville house and sat entranced.

When his father discovered the deceit, Iz threatened to run away. His father launched into a lecture. "None of the other smart boys in your class would ever do such a terrible thing. You've got to cut out the comedy. That's final." So Iz ran away, and his father temporarily disinherited him.

There is a crumbling newspaper clipping, one of Dad's first, dating back to 1900, the year of his breakaway. It tells of young Leopold, "college graduate, clubman, and author," announcing that "he had decided to give up all claim on his father's wealth and would devote the rest of his life to theatricals as playwright and actor." The story notes: "The young man has a host of friends who are astonished at his decision. That one who had everything that wealth could command should give it all up for the uncertain life before the footlights was, in their opinion, the decision of a madman."

The madman joined up with the Thurber-Nasher repertory company, a "ten-twent'-thirt' " show. They gave eleven performances a week, with a matinee every weekday except Monday, when they pitched in to hang up the scenery at their latest stop. Iz drew ten dollars a week, and his chores included passing out handbills to advertise the show. Every day was ladies' day—a handbill and a dime would buy a woman a seat.

In Haverill, Massachussetts, Dad made his bow as a solo act. He remembered that the only originality in his monologue was his entrance. "I was seated on a box in front of the drop-in-one holding a newspaper in front of my face when the curtain went up and the orchestra played "The Wearing of the Green." Then I let the paper down, and there I was in the regulation make-up of the orthodox Jewish comedian. It was a laugh. Then I began. I was booed and hissed off the stage. I never finished the monologue."

In Bangor, Maine, the Thurber-Nasher Company met its doom, nineteen weeks after it had started out. It went broke, with ten dollars and a couple of hundred undistributed handbills left in the cashbox. The Eighteenth Amendment was eighteen years ahead, but Bangor was already dry by local option. Iz found himself a job playing the piano in a recently opened speak-easy to earn his train fare back to Philadelphia.

His father treated him more as a juvenile delinquent than as a prodigal son. "With an actor in the family, how should we hold up our heads?" he demanded. "Think of the disgrace you could bring on us."

"Okay," Iz said, "so I'll change my name."

His father considered for a moment. "You can't do that," he said. "If you make a hit, nobody will know you're my son."

He set Iz up in a specially opened branch office in Boston. From there Dad traveled with a sample case filled with imitation birds, wax cherries, and ostrich plumes that he tried to sell to local millinery manufacturers. But it didn't work. The old passion consumed him again, and he committed the most heinous crime in a salesman's manual: he sold all but one of his samples and lit out for New York with the proceeds. The sample he saved was a floppy panama.

He hoped to be "The Boy with the Funny Hat." His working costume consisted of black patent-leather boots, white socks, a jacket that reached to his knees, a bow tie that reached out to both shoulders, and the hat, which he claimed he could fold into twenty-eight separate shapes. To save embarrassing his father, he changed his name by splitting "Edwin" in half.

As Ed Wynn, he played the Palace on opening night in March 1913. Ten years after that, Dad was back at the Palace again, with a sketch he wrote called *The King's Jester*, a costume piece about a clown's attempts to bring a smile to the face of a melancholy monarch.

He was playing in the same sketch at the Orpheum Theatre, Brooklyn, when on the same bill appeared Anna Held, the Swedish soprano who had been Mrs. Florenz Ziegfeld. Still keeping an eye on Anna, Ziegfeld sent Gene Buck, who who was on his staff, across to the Palace to check with Miss Held. Buck saw my father make such a hit with the audience that he took him back to see Ziegfeld.

The great man was disdainful. "I know you. I've seen you with that hat."

"Mr. Ziegfeld," Dad said solemnly, "I swear I'll throw it away and never use it again."

Ziegfeld held him to the promise and signed him for the *Follies of 1914*. He was very close to becoming a star. My mother, close to him as his shadow, was as delighted as he.

Dad never had to fight for success. Recognition came to him easily. He was so closely in step with his public that bigger billing, better contracts were almost automatic.

My mother's influence was important when Dad's income started to edge up toward a thousand dollars a week; he hadn't imagined such money, but she was at home with the luxury to be bought with that kind of salary. She could live without furs and jewelry, but she obviously enjoyed Dad's insistence that only the best from Fifth Avenue was good enough for her.

Dad had to be a star. He has told about getting a part in *The Deacon and the Lady*, the first full-length show in which he could write something longer than sketches for himself. The rehearsals were wonderful. "I ran away with it," he used to say. But Harry Kelly, who was top of the bill, complained to A. L. Erlanger, the producer, about this overdose of Wynn.

Dad was grumbling about the injustice of the cuts in a Broadway bar when, by his account, "a couple of fellows" suggested a solution: play the part as cut at the dress rehearsal, but play it as he'd written it on opening night. If anybody gave him such advice, it worked like a charm. Kelly and Erlanger were fooled at the rehearsal; when the first night came, he walked off with the show.

When he first worked for Ziegfeld, Dad began to smell big success, and he thought about having a family. My mother was a healthy girl but in no hurry to start bearing children. In those days labor pain was regarded as the price a woman paid for motherhood, and my mother was terrified of pain. As a Catholic, she had been taught that childbearing was her duty. As a woman, she was afraid, though her obstetrician, Dr. McPherson, promised her nothing would go wrong.

In *The Passing Show of 1916*, the Shubert show he opened

in after the *Follies,* Dad was the undisputed star for the first time. He was twenty-nine years old, and his imagination raced over what he might amount to—not "The Boy with the Funny Hat" or "The Rah! Rah! Boy," but as Ed Wynn. Backstage at the Winter Garden Theatre, he was nervous as a cat over the date Hilda faced at the old Lying-In Hospital at Seventeenth Street and Second Avenue. On stage, he was in another world, where there were no worries, only good, clean laughter.

During my mother's pregnancy, he had gone to his mother-in-law, Kate Keenan, to show her a diamond-and-ruby bracelet he had bought from Cartier's as a gift for my mother when the child was born. Grandma Keenan, who had become a great friend of Dad, knew her daughter's hidden feelings. "What she would like even more, Ed," she said, "is to be married as a Catholic." That was the second present he gave my mother. He promised that their child would be raised in her faith, and in the eyes of the Church my parents were married in 1916 in New York.

The orchestra at the Winter Garden had devised a plan to let Dad hear the news if the bulletin arrived while he was on stage. In the middle of the Saturday matinee on July 27, the band broke off and launched into a brand-new tune, never before played in public. Dad was halted momentarily in his tracks; then he hurried to the footlights to get the details from the orchestra leader of the telephone call Dr. McPherson had made.

He lifted a hand to quiet the buzzing audience. "My wife," he beamed, "has just had a baby. I'm the daddy of a baby boy." The orchestra struck up again with the same new melody—Gus Kahn's "Pretty Baby"—and the whole audience cheered.

At the hospital there had been something close to disaster. Fear-stricken, my mother had pulled away from the nurses in the labor room and run screaming through the door. The experience seared her; she never wanted another child.

If anybody questioned the conflict between Catholic and Jew that seethed under the calm surface of the marriage, my birth certificate gave the answer. To make certain that her son would follow in her faith, she invoked a kind of prayer in the names she chose. One half of my ancestry was erased in the name of five Catholic saints and her father. I was christened Francis Xavier Aloysius James Jeremiah Keenan Wynn.

IV

From the beginning, I was luxury's child. I was pampered, protected, swaddled, and spoiled. There was nothing I ever wanted that I wasn't given, in the shiniest and most expensive model available, from electric trains to man-sized speedboats. My father had money to burn. There was no compulsion to save, since next year would always bring more.

Before I had reached my ninth birthday, Dad was worth three million dollars. "I'm a millionaire," he used to say, "not multi- but plenty." He invested most of his available money in United States Government bonds.

We lived in growing splendor. My mother bought grand pianos, handmade furniture, Persian carpets, silverware, and mink. Dad bought diamond rings for my mother's jewel box and everything in the world for me.

We owned automobiles, boats, and houses by the pair. We were served by gardeners and governesses, chauffeurs and maids. Best of all, for a few years there was a love that embraced us all. It has sometimes been hard to remember that.

We lived on Long Island in a variety of houses, each bigger and more imposing than the one before. We started on comparatively modest planes in Laurelton and Forest Hills. We moved on to medium-sized mansions in Great Neck and reached a melancholy climax in a mausoleum that Dad called Wyngate.

Nowadays I can drive out across the East River bridges and scarcely recognize anything I see. It's hard to spot the landmarks of Long Island in the twenties. Woods and fields have been slashed to ribbons by concrete highways. Old roads where the chauffeurs would drive my mother and me to Manhattan are ugly, oil-spattered relics lined with gasoline pumps and frozen-custard stands. The beach at Wyngate is polluted and unfit for swimming any more. You search for a street and find the whole section gone, as though it never existed.

The first house of ours that I remember was a rented brown-shingled place we called "the dusty house." I have a vague memory of Dad in a brown suit kneeling to feed me with a spoon there. It stood in an expensive development known as Great Neck Estates, a few doors away from the home of Oscar Shaw. For all its comparative newness, there was something strange about the dusty house. Doors slammed in the night for no reason anybody could discover. There was talk of poltergeists.

We stayed long enough to throw a big party in January 1920, to dishonor the Eighteenth Amendment—that was the party where Mabel Normand and a punch bowl vanished together and weren't found until the following day—and then we moved to Kensington, another section of Great Neck.

It was an unusual town in an unusual era. This was Great Gatsby country; Scott Fitzgerald did, in fact, live close by. It was a racy, high-living community where prohibition didn't penetrate, and you could find a party going hot and strong almost any night of the year. I remember being taken by our friend and neighbor, Jack Curley, to see his imported French fighter, Georges Carpentier, train for his bout with

Jack Dempsey at Boyle's Thirty Acres in Jersey City. It was a local joke that Carpentier trained mostly on scotch and champagne. Everybody was amazed that he lasted four rounds before Dempsey flattened him.

The real core of our community was Broadway, a fast drive away by car and not much longer by the Long Island Railroad, which hadn't been swamped then by the real-estate developers. Actors who could afford it gravitated to Great Neck. The electoral roll read like a roster of the stars of most of the hits.

There was Thomas Meighan and Richard Barthelmess, Billy Gaxton and Charles King. This was where actors came to raise their children, the smart suburb that wasn't exactly suburbia. George M. Cohan lived there with George, Jr. So did the Joe Santleys and Joe, Jr.; Frank Craven and his son, Johnny; Jimmy and Phil Truex, of the Ernest Truex family; the Pulitzer-prize playwright Owen Davis and his next-generation namesake; Earl Benham, who often appeared with my father, and Jimmy Benham, his son. Hedda and DeWolf Hopper and their boy, Bill, rented a house. We had producers for neighbors too: Arthur Hopkins, who produced *What Price Glory?* and *Burlesque;* Sam Harris; Morris Gest, who introduced the Moscow Art Theatre to America in 1923.

The children played together, and so did their parents. If a man had no children, like Billy Gaxton and Oscar Shaw, then he played the role of uncle to the whole gang. Every Saturday during the theatre season the children were scrubbed up and put into party clothes for what we called "box parties" on Broadway.

We were scooped into whatever families' limousines were on tap for the day and chauffeured into New York for lunch. After the ice-cream sodas had been sucked dry and the candy handed out, we were ushered into boxes at a show in which one of our fathers was starring.

One week it was Oscar Shaw's turn to play host at *Oh, Kay!* Another Saturday we saw Charles King in *Hit the Deck* and drove home trying to sing "Sometimes I'm Happy, Sometimes I'm Bloo-hoo." Over the years, Dad played host more than anybody, from *The Perfect Fool* to *The Grab Bag.*

It seems there was a party for us children every day of the year. Pony rides and carousels hired for the afternoon. A scrub in the bathtub and your curls combed before you were pushed into patent-leather pumps and suits with velvet collars. Margaret Lingnau, my German governess whom we simply called Fräulein, primping me for another orgy of ice cream and pink-iced cake. Sometimes there was a reason for the party, sometimes not, except that a bunch of uninhibited parents wanted to have a good time watching their children enjoy themselves.

I think my fourth birthday party glows in my dad's memory because it symbolized for him the handful of good years when I was too young to need any identity of my own and he could see the future strictly in terms of his success and his family's dutiful enjoyment of it. It certainly was a golden, sunny day. Hired hands had put up a carousel on the well-sprinkled lawns of our Kensington house. In the double garage a bar had been set up for the adults. Dad dreamed up the idea that only children or grownups escorting a child could come. Oscar Shaw beat the ban by dressing as a child with a long blond wig, Betty-Jane shoes, sailor hat with velvet streamer, and a two-piece sailor suit.

This was the hit of the young generation's crowded social season. The Cohans came, the Cravens, the Davises. The Truex boys were there, the Santleys, and the Benhams. My mother, an excellent hostess, could homogenize the whole collection and blend Grandpa Keenan, who arrived

resplendent in white spats, with Grandma Leopold, who
hobbled around the lawn on Aunt Lizzie's arm, having a
great time.

It would have been unusual if every grownup went home
as sober as he arrived. Prohibition had been running for six
months. Everybody's thoughts had turned to liquor, in favor
of or against it. The Great Neck set could be counted as a
unanimous "aye."

Some of this story makes sense only in terms of its era,
when a bootlegger was a social necessity to adults and a
hero to kids like me. There wasn't a house around us where
contraband cocktails didn't flow. Knowing a good source of
supply was as important as having a good cook or a green-
thumbed gardener to look after the roses and rhododendrons.

I used to eavesdrop on grownups talking, and my fancy
ran wild with pictures of rumboats rolling in the swell, lowering cargoes of gin into waiting speedboats. If you belonged
to the Great Neck set, you could afford to forget about the
alky-cookers and the bathtub booze; you bought the very
best straight off the boat.

On Saturday nights the houses lit up when the big black
limousines rolled up the bluestone driveways from the
Broadway shows, bringing home the breadwinners and
guests for a weekend of rural razz-ma-tazz. Marilyn Miller,
Raymond Hitchcock, Jane Cowl, Frances Starr—they'd be
out on the Island like a shot as soon as the last-act curtains
came down. You heard saxophones bleating until daylight
with "My Rambler Rose" and "I'm Always Chasing Rainbows." The food on the buffet tables was as good as anything you could order at the Plaza, and the drinks were
better. Bronxes, sidecars, Canadian Club, and House of
Lords went down as though Pussyfoot Johnson had never
lived.

That fourth birthday of mine came not long after an im-

portant turn in Dad's career, when he helped win a strike
and, as a result, was forced into business as a kind of one-
man band: writer, lyricist, director, producer, and star of
his own shows.

He had been back with the Shuberts in their *Gaieties* at
a salary of $1,750 a week, probably the best-paid entertainer
on Broadway that year. The show had twelve months' certain booking on the road as soon as it closed in New York.
Actors Equity, the union of show business, had been struggling for recognition and, simultaneously, to win better pay
and working conditions for its members.

There was no limit in those days to the number of weeks
of unpaid rehearsal an actor or actress had to give to a show.
Sometimes a producer would call the whole thing off on the
eve of opening, and his cast went penniless.

Dad wasn't in Equity and, as a star who wrote his own
ticket within limits, he could have stayed out of the fight.
But when the strike was called he walked out with the rest
and dove into the thick of it. He paraded in the picket lines
on Broadway, stood on soapboxes making speeches at street
corners, enlisted new recruits for the strikers among stars
who were his friends.

He was Great Neck's foremost firebrand. In the midst of
it all, Dad, who liked any excuse to get friends together,
put on a party. He had signboards planted all over our house:
DO NOT DISCUSS THE STRIKE OR MENTION THOSE DAMN PRODUC-
ERS. In our living room there were strategy conferences most
days. I was ushered away by Fräulein before the talk hotted
up, but I remember Dad steaming over the injustice of the
managers and delighted by our neighbors' applause. Most
of our neighbors, that is. Some of them, like Morris Gest and
Arthur Hopkins, sat on the other side of the fence. Great
Neck was split down the middle, and friendships went up
in smoke.

The night that news of victory was telephoned to him, the whole house was in an uproar. Dad got my mother out of bed, and they both scrambled into the first clothes they could find. They ran down to take out one of the cars and play Mr. and Mrs. Paul Revere. With his finger on the horn, Dad drove through the dark streets to the Benhams' place and slid to a stop under their bedroom window. "We've won," he yelled. "The strike's over. Isn't it wonderful? We won." As Earl and Christine Benham peered bleary-eyed out their window, my mother and father whirled off to all the other houses on the long list of strikers' friends.

His own name, though, figured on a different list. He had been black-listed by the Managers' Protective Association, which swore he'd never find another job with them as long as he lived. They picked on the wrong man. No brash boy who had rocketed up the way my father had was cowed by this kind of treatment. With solid support from Mother, whose Irish blood was roused, he made up his mind to go it alone.

When he found that no manager would give him the time of day, he decided he'd produce his own show. At that point he learned that nobody could work with him; the managers threatened to black-list any actor who signed with Ed, and the new Equity contract the strike had won provided no protection against that. He couldn't get any music written either, because the managers' secondary boycott applied to songwriters too.

Dad had always made up the musical score for his vaudeville acts, so he simply sat himself down at our grand piano and wrote music and lyrics for his new show. He had been putting together his acts for years, so he also wrote the book for his revue. He got around the black-listing of actors by hiring performers from side shows and circuses, which prompted him to call his brain child *Ed Wynn's Carnival*.

It was financed on a shoestring. Dad mortgaged the house, and Mother gave him her jewels to pawn. He went off to a costume house to see what they had on their hands that he could rent cheap. If they had Japanese kimonos, then he'd write a kimono number for the show. If they were glutted with Hawaiian outfits, then he'd insert a scene that used coconut-palm skirts and ukuleles. The scenery wasn't much more than a few chairs, tables, and hastily daubed backdrops. The comic talent of Ed Wynn supplied everything else needed to make a hit.

Then he discovered that the managers' "death to Ed Wynn" vow barred him from renting a theatre. Eleven days in a row he called at Ziegfeld's office, trying to get in to see that grudging admirer. Eleven days in succession Ziegfeld sent out word by way of the receptionist that Mr. Wynn should wait. On the twelfth day, chipper as ever, Dad was going back for another try when in the lobby of the building he met B. C. Whitney, a manager from Detroit who hadn't joined the Protective Association and who had ambitions to lay hold of Ed. Dad grabbed his arm and poured out his plans for the *Carnival*. The two of them formed a partnership on the spot. After a tryout in Philadelphia the show moved into the New Amsterdam Theatre, New York, and my father's take-home pay jumped to $8,000 a week.

To mark its respect for Dad's help in the strike, Equity bought every available seat on the first night. Flo Ziegfeld sat down front. At the end of the last act, and a solid five minutes' applause, he turned to Ned Wayburn, who used to stage Ziegfeld's productions, and demanded, "Why don't you give me finales like that?"

When the time came for *Carnival* to tour, my mother took along Fräulein and me. We traveled in luxury for the next span of years until it was time to go to school. We alternated between Great Neck and the massive leather trunks we used for hotel living. My playmate was Jimmy Benham, a year younger than myself. Fräulein looked after both of us. Our playgrounds were hotel corridors. In living rooms overflowing with flower vases and Biedermeier, we were cowboys, Indians, cops, robbers, and rumboat men.

We toured Pittsburgh and Detroit, Chicago and Cincinnati, Omaha and Toronto—wherever there was a theatre and a crowd to laugh with Dad. After Fräulein had tucked me in and my parents had dressed to go out to the show, I used to fall asleep listening to the tinny music that trickled out of the Florentine radio cabinets that appeared overnight in hotel suites everywhere. I hadn't sampled it at all, so I didn't miss the rough-and-tumble life of an average small boy, with trees to shinny up and other kids to buddy with.

Up to the age of four I was Little Lord Fauntleroy, from the lace collars to the white socks, from the shoulder-long curls to the strap-over shoes. The curls, like the pampering, lasted too long for my good. I was six before I had my first haircut.

We took an elevator ride in the Edgewater Beach Hotel, Chicago, where Dad was appearing in another do-it-yourself production, *The Perfect Fool*. A well-meaning passenger patted my ringlets and said, "You have a beautiful little daughter, Mr. Wynn. Such lovely hair!"

As soon as we got up to our suite Dad delivered an ultimatum: I must be barbered immediately. Over my mother's tears I was taken downstairs for a cropping. She saved every lock of hair.

In *The Perfect Fool*, Dad made his first million dollars and latched onto the label that identified him for the rest of his career as a clown. The name was invented accidentally for him back in his *Carnival* days and stored away in his elephantine memory for future use.

On his way to the New Amsterdam one evening, he had passed by two workmen slapping up a billboard advertising John Gilbert and Norma Talmadge in *The Perfect Lovers*. He'd thought nothing more about it, but he remembered the incident, along with everything else that happened to him. At the theatre he stopped at the box office to ask about the day's business. A woman was there, trying to buy two tickets for the next evening's show. She was downcast when the clerk told her none were to be had.

"It's my mother's and father's wedding anniversary," she said. "They were dying to see Ed Wynn. They think he's a perfect fool." A bell rang in Dad's brain. This was a tag he'd make use of one day. He had the clerk sell the woman two house seats, and that was the last he heard of her.

He was physically as restless as his thoughts. Doing one thing at a time didn't satisfy him. During the run of *The Perfect Fool* he decided to take a crack at radio. Everybody was climbing on their roof tops to put up aerials, flocking to the stores to buy sets or kits for making them. He knew it was time he investigated.

Radio then was purely local entertainment. Nobody had ever heard of a network, but the government wanted to experiment with long-range transmission. The man chosen to star in the proposed two-hour tryout was my father. I just remember the hustle and bustle it caused. The program was to go out over WJZ's New Jersey transmitters, and an enormous antenna had been built in Los Angeles, designed to pick up Ed Wynn across the continent.

My mother notified Grandpa Keenan, who spent two fruitless hours by the set in his California home waiting to hear his son-in-law. In the studio Dad sweated through some *Perfect Fool* routines, delivering at the top of his squeaky voice, like a man telephoning Tibet. They picked him up in Alaska, but Frank Keenan couldn't catch a word. The jokes died a natural death somewhere in the Sierras. My grandfather, though, caught a glimpse of what the future might hold. One year later, in 1923, he wrote:

"Within a period of time comparatively brief, we shall be sitting in our own private houses with our own private picture screen, our projector, our phonograph and amplifier, and on our roof our own set of wireless aerials. Sitting there in our library chairs, we shall be able to see and hear, without moving, every word or sound or scene or situation of a show that is being staged in actuality perhaps thousands of miles away. . . . That is the future of the picture, part of it. I do not think it will wipe out the motion picture. I believe that a new angle in presentation will be developed here, as yet unthought of." He saw it all except the name. He didn't guess it would be called television.

The fortune Dad was piling up set off a burst of social ambition in him. He had reached the top as an entertainer. Now it seemed he wanted to outshine everybody else as the landed proprietor of one of the most fantastic houses in the community of Great Neck. He bought the place that he rechristened Wyngate.

He wanted the best of everything for himself, mother, and me. His attitude was: "Now we're all going to enjoy the very finest things money can buy." Wyngate was the highest he ever flew.

It was as big as a palace. Besides the private beach, it had hothouses, acres of lawn, rooms by the dozen. It needed six servants to run it and my mother's full-time attention as chatelaine, hostess, and lady almoner. Our new neighbors were the Walter Chryslers and nearby lived the Graces, the shipping family. Maybe they liked living in mansions without warmth and intimacy. We hadn't that kind of taste. Wyngate was a monster.

It's a dark unhappy name to me. My childhood came to an end there before it really got started. It was the saddest place we ever lived in.

V

At first it seemed not too different from what we had been
growing used to. Mother would have Christine Benham and
other friends over regularly to brighten up the rooms with
affection and fun. They spent half the day on our beach
sunning themselves, while luncheon and drinks were served
and the women gossiped over the crossword puzzles that
had become the latest fashion in killing time.

I had started going to public school in Great Neck. I was
driven there and collected by the chauffeur or, on his day
off, the estate superintendent, who lived over the garages
and also looked after the hothouses, where Mother raised
orchids.

In the evenings, while Dad worked, she sometimes wore a
flower. She sometimes sat at the piano in the music room to
play for me. You could tell she'd had a wonderful touch,
but she'd let it go since her marriage. She sang for me too.
"Mighty Lak' a Rose" was my favorite; she'd sung that when
she toured with my aunt Fuff. Like her playing, her voice
was unpracticed, but it was the sweetest sound in my world.

This innocent prelude to tragedy couldn't have lasted
more than six months. Exactly when the trouble began it is
impossible to tell. It started undetectably, like the first stone

skittering down a mountain to touch off an avalanche. My
mother's behavior began to change.

There were moments during the day when she was suddenly silent. I would say, "Mother, may I stay up for five
more minutes before Fräulein takes me to bed?" No answer.
If I touched her hand and repeated my question, I'd get
a smile and her reply. Then the moments of brooding got
longer.

"Snap out of it, Hilda," Christine Benham said briskly.
"You look so glum today. Is anything wrong?"

My mother smiled and shook her head. Her friends tried
hard to bring her back to the gaiety they'd enjoyed, but she
eluded them. The silence spread like a stain.

Fräulein told me increasingly, "Don't bother your mother,
Keenan." There was no special reason why I should, only to
look for daily tokens of her love, which were harder to find.
But there were Fräulein and the chauffeur and the other
servants. The house was big enough for me never to see
my mother, if it came to that. I started eating without her,
and I slept on a screened-in porch away from her room.

Dad led a double life. At home he was worried over Hilda.
At work, in *The Grab Bag*, he was perfecting the lisp, the
simper, the lunatic inventions that were his followers' delight. He had the ability to switch his thinking from reality
to his rainbow-colored humor, the way you snap a light on
and off.

He spent hours dreaming up the gag of the inch-long
harmonica, which he demonstrated to the audience in Act
One of *The Grab Bag*: "I shall now oblige you, I hope, with
a musical solo." After a bar or two of blowing, the harmonica got lost inside his mouth, and it seemed as though
he'd swallowed it. For the rest of the show, he'd stand by
the wings and give a nervous cough. An out-of-sight stage-
hand simultaneously blew a blast on a full-size harmonica,

which thereby seemed to wheeze in Dad's stomach. It was a gag that stopped the show.

My mother grew steadily more remote, more isolated inside herself. Our friends found their own explanations. The reasons they offered ran from her sheer solitude in the acreage of Wyngate to her unhappiness at being overshadowed by Dad. I think both factors were important.

She had been contented enough until we moved. She'd been able to handle her household, encourage her husband, give her personal attention to me. The size of Wyngate intimidated her. To run the place, she needed more servants than she could ever find. She had to be sterner, more demanding than her nature allowed if she was going to keep up with people like the Chryslers. And she needed more help from Dad than she ever got. As the magnesium inside him flared up, he had precious little time to give her.

It was never easy to live with Dad. He was a man who talked more than he listened. In any company he was the dominating personality. He considered his judgment infallible, seldom listened to any advice that ran counter to his convictions. He was self-made and changed inside by the effort it took.

Looking back, I can see what appalled my mother. She was sure she was intrinsically smarter than Dad, a bigger human being with more talent. But he was the one who had made the reputation, and he was the one who got the applause.

There were not many people he had reason to listen to any longer. Grandpa Leopold had died a year earlier, with the puzzle of how young Iz had made a go of it unsolved in his mind. He died of cancer after long, painful treatment at the hands of the best specialists Dad could engage. One of his last thoughts was that other people had to be spared what he had suffered by way of treatment. "Get me a revolver," this kind and gentle man whispered to Dad. "I have to kill the doctor." Grandma Leopold had to be provided for now; Dad rented an apartment for her overlooking the ocean at Atlantic City.

Grandpa Keenan alternated between his stage appearances and making motion pictures with his own production company. Now and again the smoke of his coronas drifted through Wyngate, but Dad had outgrown his need to look up to Frank Keenan.

In that year when I was nine years old, the threads of love between my parents began to twist. Even I could see it. To save me from the unhappiness it caused, Dad decided to send me off to school. Easier said than achieved. He'd no alma mater beyond a Philadelphia high school, and he wanted me to be a "gentleman." He had my name down on no waiting lists, because he'd always planned to keep me at home.

But luck was with him—and me. In Hawthorne, New York, he found a place that seemed suitable and would accept me. I was admitted to the Harvey School, which still stands on sixty or more acres of woodland close to where the Taconic State Parkway slices north now toward Albany.

I felt like something pathetic that fall day when we took the train from Grand Central Station up to the little village of Hawthorne for me to be presented at Harvey. My mother had come to a happy break in her illness; she and Fräulein took me to school. Dad was miles away, touring.

The three of us bundled into a taxi at the station and drove the mile or so to Harvey. The school, with its lawns and ranks of elms, looked as if it had stood for a hundred years—solid, calm, and completely alien. I'd never suspected such places existed. It was as big a mystery to me as its motto: *Scientia et Veritas*—Knowledge and Truth. I didn't

know much about either one when my mother and I kissed
good-by, with tears from us both, and I stumbled blindly
up the worn brick steps of Harvey Hall and tapped timidly
on the headmaster's door.

Compared to my schoolmates, I was a freak, a creature
from Broadway, and as remote as a Bantu. They were followers in a bland tradition that would carry them on to
Andover and Choate, Kent and Exeter before it bore them,
equally surely, to the best fraternities at Harvard, Dart-
mouth, Yale, and Princeton. They were safe in their patterns,
these impressive young men, aged nine to fifteen, with names
like Sayres and Stickney, Pentecost and Holmes.

I was show business. I was the first-born Wynn, and the
son of Leopold. I was desperately homesick.

By contrast with most fathers, Dad was an upstart, "little
rich." They were bankers, lawyers, judges, diplomats, men
born to money and prestige status. The advantage he held
over them was that he could move them to laughter with a
tilted eyebrow, control their emotions as easily as he hit notes
on a piano. But like the rest of the world that knew him
only as an entertainer, they had no idea of the man inside
Ed Wynn.

I tasted discipline for the first time in my life. The rules
weren't harsh, but they were strict: be punctual, be attentive,
be polite. To keep a touch of Wyngate I had permission to
room with six other boys on the sleeping porch. I blubbered
myself to sleep for weeks until Mabel Carter, the old headmaster's wife, took pity and made a special friend of me.

My mother stayed well, and she went on tour again with
Dad to get away from the overwhelming atmosphere of
Wyngate. By Thanksgiving she was in Omaha. By Harvey
rules, I couldn't get leave to join her. So for three days she
rode the train alone, to spend the day at school. I had become
very anxious to be one of the fellows and hide my oddness

under a camouflage of conformity. But the sight of my mother spoiled it all. She found some peace in the hills of the Saw Mill River Valley that day. She didn't want to leave. We were heartbroken all over again at having to say good-by.

I was still too young and stupid to be more than dimly aware of changes in my mother. When Christmas vacation came and I went off with her to join Dad in Lexington, Kentucky, for Christmas Day, I still believed in Santa Claus, firmly and literally. On Christmas Eve, aboard the train, I sat in pajamas and dressing gown waiting to be tucked into bed in our suite.

"Did Santa Claus get on the train?" I asked the Pullman porter. "Are you positive he'll find me and bring some presents?"

My mother laughed and hugged me. "Of course he did, darling. Santa Claus always does. Doesn't he, porter?" The porter nodded, beaming.

That was the last Christmas Santa Claus ever found me. There were other Christmases, more piles of presents from every fancy emporium in the forty-eight states. But the gift of family love was never to be discovered under our tree again.

My mother had always made a wonderful Christmas for us. The trimmings and the packages were lavish, as you'd expect from the Ed Wynns, but it was more than a spending spree. She made Christmas a significant occasion. We sang carols by the fire and listened to her tell the story of the first Christmas. There'd be trains from Schwarz running over yards of track, cowboy outfits, skates, building blocks, wagons, construction sets, cars, popguns, balloons, candy canes. The neighbors' children would crowd in to exchange presents, with shrieks of laughter and whoops of joy. But under all the fun, we were taught to remember the first Christmas and the Man who created it.

I spent only six months at Harvey. My mother wanted me home, and Dad made up his mind to take me out as abruptly as I'd been put in. There was scarcely time to realize I was leaving, apparently forever, at the Easter vacation, but I'd been there long enough to feel sick at heart. I'd discovered my own kind and a sense of belonging that I couldn't explain.

My mother was ill again, more seriously than before. Too shaky to travel, she saw herself deserted in a house she hated, with her husband constantly away and her son off in boarding school. Harvey didn't permit weekend leave, and Dad appreciated that she needed family as much as a doctor's care. I was the present he tried to give her, and I could feel only resentment start to stir.

I was back in the routine of morning delivery and afternoon pickup from the Kensington public school. My abysmal ignorance continued, deepened because nobody attempted to explain what was really happening in my family.

I remember visiting the chauffeur's wife when she was pregnant. On the way home in the car, I asked her husband sympathetically, "What's wrong with your wife, Harry? Is she sick like my mother?"

One night my mother was carried off by ambulance to New York, to enter a hospital on Lexington Avenue. On my dad's instructions I was taken the next day and every day to visit her, sometimes with one servant, sometimes with another. I remember her room being filled with fresh flowers sent in by Dad. I recall the hot summer and the gritty boredom of riding into Pennsylvania Station, then catching a cab to the hospital. She looked as young and beautiful as she'd ever looked, but there was a listlessness about her.

Those were not the strongest impressions I carried away.

What I felt most strongly was bitterness at the upset to my own life; I had the hangdog reaction of a spoiled child who hoped he could cut short his daily visit in time to get home for a swim before dark.

Sometime in 1926, two years after he bought it, Dad gave up Wyngate and his dream of living like the big rich. He sold the place for $400,000, and we moved back into the Kensington house that nobody had wanted to take off his hands. He had wakened to part of my mother's problem. None of us knew it was too late to do much good.

VI

It was 1927, and Dad had opened that summer in George White's *Manhattan Mary*. At this Saturday matinee I sat with a bunch of new schoolmates, and we laughed ourselves sick. There was something about a gangster, for instance, who slouched into a speak-easy and asked the shivering waiter what was on the menu. The waiter, who was Ed, lisped a suggestion about trying the ladyfingers or the jelly roll.

"My God," snarled the thug, "I'm so hungry I could eat a horse."

Dad ran off through the swing doors and came back tugging a live horse. It took minutes for the yells of laughter to die so he could say his next line: "With mustard or ketchup?" The audience howled again.

I was very proud of him. I wore a gaudy blue uniform trimmed with epaulets and gold braid an inch thick, like the rest of our company. We had marched down the aisle to our seats after we'd scrambled out of the hired buses that brought us from Ossining, where we were all in boarding school. We were cadets and presumably gentlemen at a gloomy dump called St. John's Military Academy, run by three generations of a family of headmasters, where my father had enrolled me.

Maybe some kids liked the place, not me. From the drills to the uniform, it was a sad place. When I think of St. John's I think of treacle, which flowed over every slice of boiled pudding served on the bare plank tables for every dessert.

If we had lived on Coke and candy bars, I'd still have been gloomy. More changes at home had shaken up my existence. Dad chose St. John's because I could get away for every weekend. Every Friday night I took the train down to Grand Central to spend two nights visiting my mother. That part of the treatment continued.

That spring Dad had hit on the idea of getting us all out of the country to make a fresh start, build up my mother's health and start us seeing straight again. In April we'd sailed in the old Cunard four-stacker, S.S. *Olympic,* to spend most of the summer abroad until Dad had to get back for the show.

Because I would be missing out on several weeks of school between April and June—and my education was flimsy enough without that—Dad hired a tutor, a Mr. Resinol from Columbia University, to tackle the impossible job of piercing my ignorance. Mr. Resinol sailed with us and, talking four or five languages, showed us the sights. He had a rough time of it, but he was well paid—Dad didn't stint on spending.

We stayed in the best hotels, ate the best food, visited the best places, living like king, queen, and crown prince. I thought the whole trip had a golden glow; we were together as a family, typical tourists, and we seemed as happy as ice-cream cones. I didn't know then that Dad took us to London so that he could see psychiatrists there about my mother's health. Or that we went to Rome for a private audience with the Pope because Dad hoped that this might help my mother's health where doctors had failed.

We sailed home again in the *Olympic* to a decisive breakup in my parents' marriage.

Dad started rehearsing for *Manhattan Mary*, and my mother was apparently well again. She was still quiet and withdrawn, but she gave no signs of being under stress. No signs, anyway, that a schoolboy could detect.

Dad had gone to Pittsburgh to open the new show, and I was living alone with my mother when illness hit her again. I didn't know what to do. Our friend and neighbor, Joe Santley, hurried in to take charge. He got Dad on the telephone in Pittsburgh. "Hilda's sick and Keenan's very upset about it. What can I do to help out?"

I suppose the marriage had really ended much earlier. The flicker of vitality we'd glimpsed in Europe was no more than an afterglow. Both of them accepted the end as inevitable. My mother had to choose between Dad and a kind of darkness in her heart; the choice went against him. The summer's night when Joe Santley called, Dad was confronted with a similar decision: between the show and his wife, between the hilarious thing called *Manhattan Mary* and the woman—she was thirty-seven—that he'd adored.

"I can't leave the show right now, Joe," he said. "If you'll arrange to send Keenan out to me, I'll take care of him."

So my mother was carried off to the hospital, and I was sent to Pittsburgh. From there Dad put me in St. John's.

When my mother was well enough to be discharged, she moved into the penthouse he had rented at 3 West Fiftieth Street, closed down the Kensington house. Our Long Island era was almost finished. Some of the massive furniture was crammed into the new apartment, which was a box room compared with Wyngate.

In the future when Dad played New York, he stayed in hotels. If we couldn't live together, we'd have to get along apart. He'd pay all the bills and cede me to my mother every weekend from St. John's. That was the life of Ed Wynn when he played *Manhattan Mary*, which a lot of his admirers rate as his funniest show of all.

When Mother moved into the apartment, we got along famously. Away from Ed, she had the manner of a new woman. She couldn't do enough to make me happy. Every meal at weekends was chosen because I'd like it. In my room everything was arranged and laid out for my tastes: model boats, games of all kinds, clothes, hobbies, the whole collection.

One weekend we went to the opening of Palisades Amusement Park across the river in New Jersey. I dragged my laughing, handsome mother onto the Cyclone ride, the scenic railway that dipped and dove and rattled us into delighted terror at the prospect of being flung clear into the Hudson. And then the cars stuck, and we had to pick our way down to the ground along a catwalk, holding hands and happy as school kids.

Another weekend when I came home, my mother said, "We have to go to Washington, Keenan. Grandpa's down there, and you'll have to help bring him back."

Frank Keenan was booked at the Palace, starting the next Monday. He'd spent the week just passed playing Washington, where he'd encountered some drinking companions he didn't want to leave. My mother's problem was how to pry him loose to keep the Palace date. This kind of situation wasn't rare. Grandpa Keenan was fond of me, so I was cast as a Judas sheep to lead him where he had to go.

In Washington we went straight to his dressing room and found he'd been drinking for days. My mother nudged me into action.

"Come back to New York with me, Grandpa, then tomorrow you can take me to the zoo in Central Park, and we can feed the squirrels and everything."

He smiled benignly. "Boy, stay here for the weekend with me. We're going to see the sights of our capital: the Washington Monument, the Smithsonian Institution, the halls of Congress——"

"Maybe we could even have a ride around the park in a horse and carriage; I'd like that."

"—the White House and all the other splendors right here. Why go to New York?"

"I like it better there," I said meekly. He was half persuaded, enough to let Mother hurry him to his hotel to pack. I helped her load him inside for the cab ride to Union Station. While she went off to check the bags and buy the tickets, I stayed with Grandpa, who was holding himself up with an iron hand gripping my shoulder.

Through the crowd came a priest, a quiet, middle-aged man. Grandpa Keenan steered us over to him, staring like a hawk through his pince-nez. In his best organ tones Grandpa said, "Father, would you be good enough to direct me to the nearest whore house?" Then my mother arrived to offer a brisk apology to the red-faced priest and usher us onto a waiting train.

At the end of the St. John's school year, it was my turn to spend some time with Dad. On the way to Atlantic City, Dad turned off the highway at Toms River, New Jersey, to call on an old friend, Dave Marion. Talking with him, Dad got the idea that he and I should have a vacation together on the spot, fishing in the Toms River. He took me shopping for outdoor clothes, and we spent two wonderful weeks. While we were away, Grandpa Keenan and his third wife, Leah, visited my mother and tried to patch things up. My grandfather telephoned Dad the news that his daughter was willing to try another reconciliation. I remember talking on the phone to her, popping with delight because I could say, "Dad is coming home with me." We all met at the apartment.

We spent the early part of that summer at Larchmont, New York. Out of gratitude for the turn for the better our lives had taken, Dad splurged on a speedboat, a twenty-two-foot Chris-Craft Kaydet with a 125-horsepower Chrysler engine.

My grandfather and Leah came to stay with us, and we took them out in the Kaydet. We went to Playland in Rye, brand-new at that time, and, in our roles as normal, happy people, spent a great day there. I got Grandpa onto the scenic railway, but we hadn't any catwalk climbing to do, which was his good luck—he was then seventy years old.

Like run-of-the-mill rich, we moved on for some weeks at Martha's Vineyard, where my mother had spent summers as a child, and then on again to Nantucket, the White Elephant Inn, which was jammed with summer people chattering about the sailboat races and what would the Model-A Ford look like and what new fortunes you could make in the big bull market. Dad wasn't tempted to switch into anything riskier than his government bonds.

That fall I was taken back into the Harvey School. My mother, armed with the clothes list, took me off to buy a full set of new gear from blue cap, dark blue Sunday suit, "six suits light underwear," to "one pair black shoes for dress wear." It was exciting and wonderfully reassuring. Going back was like going back home.

In the taxi crunching up the gravel driveway, I felt bewildered that nothing had changed. The big brass bell still hung in the apple tree outside Harvey Hall, rung to mark out the periods of the day. Outside the office—sharp turn left as you went in—hung the engraving of an old steam packet that hundreds of boys had stood and studied as they waited for mail. There was a new headmaster, Herbert Carter, who had followed his father in the appointment.

Nothing else had changed, only me. Since my first brief stay, I seemed to have lived a lifetime. It was hard to believe I'd been a blubbering kid before. This time I was going to be a regular fellow, which was the very best kind.

Boarding-school routine took over, like a massage easing stiff muscles. We climbed out of bed at six-thirty every morning. Under a master's eye we dashed into a cold shower. We dressed, then came breakfast, then came prayers of a non-denominational variety. We started lessons by eight-thirty and didn't finish until eleven hours later.

Lights out at eight-thirty, and you'd better look sharp, Wynn, or you'll get another demerit. Too many of those, and you had to pace the gravel walks around the lawns in front of Harvey Hall, number of times around decided by the gravity of your crimes. I made the rounds on some occasions, but that never bothered me. I was home, and I was happy.

I picked up a reputation as the class clown. If you wanted to hear the best jokes, you came to Wynn. They were Dad's jokes, passed on to me by letter or telephone. He made another contribution toward making friends for me: he invited the entire school dramatic club, of which I was a member, into New York for a Saturday matinee.

He hired the buses to bring forty-five boys and half a dozen grownups down from Hawthorne. He stood us all lunch at Reuben's. Then into one of his monologues he ad-libbed the name of every boy and Herbert Carter. We had a fine time.

At the end of the day one of my new pals, Coot Draper, shook his head in wonder at the sheer opulence of the treat. Draper came from a North Carolina family with as much

breeding as money, but not the obvious kind of money the
Wynns threw around.

"Your father is a most magnanimous man," he said. "Why,
I bet today must have cost him at least *twenty dollars.*"

On Parents' Day, Dad drove out in spectacular style to
play baseball, parents against boys. He stopped the game
by getting everybody helpless with laughter at his horsing
around the diamond. He sent out autographed pictures of
himself to any boy who asked, customarily inscribed, "To
my son Keenan's school chum; sincerely, Ed Wynn."

In the outside world that we explored only at vacation
time, the earthquake had hit Wall Street. It had no more
significance for us at first than a flood on the Yangtze River.
Dad's cautious investing paid off in a bank balance that
stayed healthy. On the eve of the crash my mother and
father moved into an elegant co-operative apartment on East
End Avenue to take another shot at living together. They
weathered the next years' economic storms without any
trouble. It was the emotional hurricanes that swamped them.

New enrollments declined at Harvey; fees were slower
coming in. The fact that Dad could pay promptly and
in full may have saved me once or twice from being
invited to depart. As the class clown I hadn't much time for
study. "In some cases," Herbert Carter told Dad at the end
of the first school year, "he has done more acting than studying." I was more interested in building tree houses in the
woods and ducking out to the off-limits hot-dog stand, which
was the height of sinful living.

With my great pal, George Olin Walbridge III, I was
wrapped up in a semi-secret society we formed, based on the
novels of Alexander Dumas, especially *The Man in the Iron
Mask* and *The Three Musketeers.* There was a rival organization, led by George Swift Trow, dedicated to Howard
Pyle and the Knights of the Round Table.

I was intent on being *liked* and just as conscious of the need to be discreet about it. I didn't want to trade on Dad's reputation; I had to be liked on my account, not on his. There was some snobbery in this. Every boarding school is to some degree a snob school. Perhaps I inherited a Jewish sensitivity. Anyway, I clowned around and plunged into any mildly illicit activity that came along to prove I was as regular as any son of a gentile of greater size in the world than Dad.

Presumably Herbert Carter saw some merit in what I was trying to do. The fee alone wouldn't have persuaded him to keep me there. He wasn't that kind of man. One boy, whose name as an adult decorates café-society gossip columns, was expelled as a juvenile reprobate, though his grandmother donated a whole new house to Harvey as an argument for holding onto him.

Mr. Carter was a Rhodes Scholar whose creed was character. He was convinced the years between nine and fourteen were none too early for instilling a sense of direction in a boy. The means he used ranged from cold showers to hobby clubs devoted to music, model trains or fly-tying. I wished he had been my father. He was a demigod to me.

Herbert Carter and Ed Wynn collided head on. Dad never won a battle, but he never quit trying. What he fought for was special treatment for himself and me. By letter, telephone call, or personal visit, he was forever wheedling or sounding off at the master to let me off the leash and skip off to New York. He wanted to have me with him as consolation in his continually difficult marriage. He wanted to make me a Wynn and not a Keenan.

But Herbert Carter cared more about the future of boys than the problems of their parents. To all the pleas and pressures Dad got the same answer: "I am sorry, I cannot

allow Keenan to be excused from school next Wednesday."
Or: "No, it is impossible for him to go to town on Sunday."

Though I hadn't much to say to him or do with him, Dad
went to extraordinary lengths in this peculiar courtship. For
days on end he'd telephone every day from wherever he
was traveling. He'd drive two or three hundred miles on a
Sunday to spend an hour, a grudging hour on my part,
with me. One winter's day he pushed on through a blizzard
from upstate New York. His car was one of the first equipped
with mechanical windshield wipers instead of the old hand-
operated variety. That's what made an otherwise impossible
journey feasible. He arrived tense and cold. I felt no pity,
which isn't a schoolboy's emotion.

When he got no answers to his letters he tried humor
to bridge the silence. Once, away somewhere on the road, he
wrote himself a long, affectionate letter about Harvey and
mailed it to me for signature. I thought, "Who's he trying
to kid?" I was turning away from him for a lot of reasons,
all centering on the secret war inside our family.

At Harvey I ran into anti-Semitism for the first time. It
happened during my first stay there as a ten-year-old.

I had been enrolled a Catholic. When Mother filled in
the application blank she underlined that fact. Religious
affiliation? "Catholic," she wrote. Church attended? "St. Patrick's Cathedral (Roman Catholic)." As one of the six or
seven of my faith at Harvey, I enjoyed some advantages.
On Sundays we piled into a Model-T station wagon, driven
by Mr. Healey, the Irish math master, to go off to Mass in
Pleasantville, another village close to Hawthorne. Getting
away from school gave us the chance to load up on newspapers and candy before we were driven home.

On the first Sunday morning after one Christmas vacation,
I was just climbing into the station wagon to join the little
band of the faithful for Mass, when a boy, whose name is

not important, stuck out a foot, pushed me in the chest, and jeered, "You can't come with us; you're a Jew."

There was only one immediate answer in Harvey's code. I reached into the wagon and dragged him out. We rolled over on the gravel in our blue Sunday suits, beating the daylights out of each other.

Herbert Carter stormed out to see what was wrong. My tormentor and I were shuddering with tears and temper and a peculiar kind of pain. We were hauled into the headmaster's study with a demand for explanations. When he listened to our stories, Herbert Carter grew as pale as we were. His fist clenched and unclenched on his big desk. In his precise Princeton accent he snapped, "It will not do. It will not do at all."

He ordered the whole Catholic contingent in to hear a brief, pungent lecture on the evil of intolerance. Then Herbert Carter, scholar and gentleman, loaded us into the station wagon and drove us personally to Mass.

VII

It took me years as a man to recognize the truth of what I was. Then it was something I remembered Grandpa Leopold saying that gave me the clue. He died when I was eight years old, but my mother had often entrusted me to his care, and I clearly remember Dad lifting me up as a very small boy and boasting to my grandfather about how smart I was. The old man shook his head. "Different blood," he said.

At Harvey I used to try to puzzle it out, looking for an answer to "Who am I?" The full-lipped face I saw in mirrors was Dad's face, my face. But I was Catholic. I'd known no other religion since my mother taught me prayers, and I went to catechism class as soon as I was old enough to qualify. I received my First Communion in Great Neck. I went to Mass every Sunday with my mother when she was well enough, and she sent me with the chauffeur to make sure I got there when she was ill.

Catholicism was a religion of fear to me as a child. What stayed in my mind was the brimstone, the danger of eternal damnation, not the love. When I started being instructed by the priests, I was a kid in a small town on Long Island, where a great building boom had long been under way. The church was in the old village of Great Neck, up the hill from the Kensington area. The congregation was mostly made up of Polish and Italian laborers and their families, who had been pouring into the place since the turn of the century. Perhaps because of their needs, the teaching that children got there lingered on the themes of hell-fire and purgatory. I could almost smell the smoke.

The Pleasantville church we went to from Harvey was another little place where the same old-line blasts from the inferno colored the instruction of children. Much the same reason applied: Westchester was growing fast on the muscles of immigrant laborers. I was never introduced to what can be called modern Catholicism. I am sure Bishop Fulton Sheen knows just what I mean. I am equally certain that if I'd met someone like him when I was seven or eight my life would have been a lot different.

As it was, I took in bigotry through the pores, as my mother had before me. There were people on their knees beside us in both Great Neck and Pleasantville whose instinct was to spit at the name of a Jew. So what was I supposed to think of myself, half gentile, half Jew? And what in the name of God was I supposed to think of my father? I shrugged off the problem by having as little as possible to do with Dad.

It was away from school, during the summer vacation of 1929, that anti-Semitism hit me again. My mother had spent such a good summer at Nantucket the previous year that she wanted to go back. Dad agreed, and we packed off, expecting to spend most of the season there. I'd developed an appetite for any kind of boat, so Mother thought she would enroll me in a yacht club with the other kids whose parents were summering on the island.

I was thirteen years old, and I was blackballed as a Jew. The man whose sensitive gentile stomach revolted at the

thought of my presence was in show business, depending
for his living on a profession that owes a lot of its laughter
to Jews like Phil Silvers, George Burns, Jack Benny, Groucho
Marx; owes many of its songs to Irving Berlin, George Gersh-
win, Al Jolson; owes great stage roles to men like Paul Muni
and Edward G. Robinson.

I can today forgive the blackball for myself, but not
for its effect on my mother. God love her, she was tremendously hurt by the slur. Her Irish temper exploded.
"That's all," she snapped when the news came. "Out! We're
going to leave Nantucket right now." By morning we had
gone back to New York.

It was a relief when that vacation ended and I returned
to Harvey, where I knew the rules and could hold my own
against anybody. When I tried, I could usually land about
halfway in class. But good or bad as a scholar, I was myself,
Keenan Wynn. Dad could be forgotten.

Meantime, he kept up his struggle to get privileges from
Herbert Carter. Herbert Carter to Ed Wynn, May 22, 1930:
"I must have definite assurance that both of you believe
Keenan's schoolwork and his school life to be the most
serious thing for him at this time."

Herbert Carter to Ed Wynn, April 28, 1931: "I think he
does not know the difference between being on and off the
stage."

Herbert Carter to Ed Wynn, June 19, 1931: "I would
recommend for his development that you give him as much
responsibility as you can. It would be the best thing in the
world for him if he could feel that he was taking some
weight off your shoulders."

What with my indifference and the lectures the headmaster read to him, Dad developed a persecution complex.
He half believed that Carter singled out Ed Wynn and son
for harsh treatment. My usual end-of-year report card drove

him frantic: "He cared little for schoolwork . . . Clever, superficial, not interested in his work . . . His attitude in class is always looking for a break and taking it when it comes."

"How can they possibly treat you like this, Keenan?" he asked at vacation time. "Can't they give you better marks than these?"

Once his resentment led him into a showdown with Herbert Carter. Dad had come to New York to spend his forty-fourth birthday. He knew my mother couldn't share in any celebration. So he wrote another begging letter in advance asking for me to be given the day in town with him. He arrived late at the apartment. No Keenan and no reply to his letter.

He picked up the telephone in a rage to call Carter: "It's unfair and unjust to deprive me of my son on my birthday."

"Mr. Wynn," the headmaster said coldly, "you know we make no exceptions for any boy. I am sorry. Good night."

Dad couldn't fight back. Much as he wanted me with him, he had to keep me at Harvey. He wanted me raised as he had never been, protected from the world entirely, brought up in cotton and with kid gloves. Besides, if I left Harvey, there was no place I could go.

Nowadays a boy who fails there gets a certificate of honorable dismissal to soften the blow for his parents. In my day a sterner rule applied: "No graduation, no diploma." When graduation day arrived for the class of '31, I'd no hope of glory. I lounged at Dad's side through the ceremonies, not giving a damn for the speechmaking or the pained look on his face.

I could grin; Dad couldn't. But he had to disguise his wounds by pretending I'd been a casualty too. Back in the apartment that night, he spelled it out in a last letter to Herbert Carter: "The graduation-day exercises broke his heart. Mine, too. I think you could at least have mentioned Keenan's name. I almost regret Keenan's years at school because of this terrible slight. It sure hurt us all."

The truth was that I'd grown a thick skin that made me proof against any such injury. It was like scar tissue that had covered old wounds. Those wounds were inflicted by my mother, whom I loved and went on loving.

During my school years my parents finally gave up trying to work out their marriage. My father left my mother to the secretive world into which she retreated more and more often. She abandoned him in her heart, though she was always asking for news of him from me. "How is that prince of good fellows, your father?" she was always asking, not intending it as any kind of sneer.

She retained a strong love for him, though she rejected him for what he'd turned out to be—a distant man who lived for applause. In her sickness, her despair drove her to dreadful things.

None of this was a secret to me any longer, but it was a secret that had to be kept when I was at Harvey. I felt strangely different from my companions. A sentence I read in *David Copperfield* could just as well have been written about me: "I was so conscious of having passed through scenes of which they could have no knowledge, and of having acquired experiences foreign to my age, appearance and condition as one of them, that I half believed it was an imposture to come there as an ordinary little schoolboy."

There was one scene in particular.

It was a Saturday morning, and it was an empty one because I hadn't anybody to go out with and nowhere to go. I was home at 3 West Fiftieth Street on a vacation from school. My mother and I were alone, she in her bedroom, I killing time over a game of solitaire. She was in the middle of one of the attacks that destroyed all judgment and self-control. When I heard the door of her room open I looked up.

Illness had never spoiled her looks. She was a ruin only in her heart and mind. She stood in the doorway, tall and imperious in a silk robe that gave her the appearance of being on stage in some classic tragedy.

She stared at me for a moment, studying the face in which she could see only her husband. At that moment she utterly disdained him. Her voice was deep and husky when she pointed at me.

"You Jew," she said, "with your father's lips."

Part Two

VIII

Until I was fifteen I remained in blank ignorance about the world and its normal people. I had never bought anything so simple and basic as a loaf of bread; such jobs were left to servants. I didn't know that somebody had to take care of things like laundry; in my life up to then you just opened a drawer and there was a clean shirt.

My feet were kept a mile off the ground, and my head was up in the clouds. I had no idea of ever providing for myself or earning a living. "You don't have to bother about the future," Dad always told me. "I'll take care of you."

Then suddenly, with outside help, I could feel firm ground under my feet for the first time. I reached a real crossroads, and I began to grow up. It came about as the result of a ride I took in the second of three speedboats Dad bought before my eighteenth birthday. This was a 28-footer, successor to the Kaydet.

By this time I was competent enough to handle a boat and even to qualify for a charter captain's license soon after, but my mother was afraid to have me go out alone. She usually sent the family chauffeur along. He hated the job, and I did my best to make him miserable. On this day I was bored, as ever, with my mother's insistence that Charlie, who had no boating experience, had to ride with me. I let him fumble the boat on some rocks in Little Hell Gate as one means of convincing her that what I needed as a companion was somebody who really knew something about boating. We had to sit and wait for a passing speedboat to tow us clear.

In the boat, the *Jackie B.*, was a man who, in a few eye-opening weeks, turned out to be a Dutch uncle to me, with some qualities of philosopher and hell-raiser thrown in. His name was Hector Alexander, a peppy Scotsman a few years short of forty, who worked as a test driver for the Cadillac Motor Company.

He told me later: "I heard it was Ed Wynn's son stuck on those rocks, and I thought, 'That's a damn-fool thing to do. The kid can't know his head from a hole in the ground.' "

I was happy to tell my mother, "Charlie put us on the rocks today." She knew Duffy's Yacht Landing and the club at the Seventy-ninth Street dock, so she telephoned there to ask Captain Sullivan, who worked at the place, to recommend somebody to work as our boatman.

He recommended an ex-broker's man, Dick Powell, who had lost his job in Wall Street as a result of the crash. Mother interviewed Dick, and he was put on Dad's payroll as a kind of nursemaid and boatman combined.

On one of our first outings together, Dick drove me to North Beach, a Long Island airport, to meet some of his friends. There we were, an oddly assorted pair, a kid overflowing with egotism founded on a phony sense of superiority, and his chaperon, out to justify his pay. Up on the wing of an S-39 Sikorsky seaplane stood a small, trim guy in overalls, working on the engine.

"This is Hector Alexander, my brother-in-law," Dick said. "Hec, this is Ed Wynn's son."

A sardonic face looked down on us, unimpressed. "What does that make me—an Elk?"

I felt a jolt inside. Except at school, I'd been exposed to nothing but the sycophants, neighbors, and nodders who surrounded Dad. I'd been stifled by servants, lackeys, and men who deliberately abased themselves to flatter him. They weren't motivated by fear of him, because he didn't generate that at all, but simply because he was the boss, the top dog. As the boss's son, I got the kid-glove treatment too. I imagine it's a universal situation, as common in the corner delicatessen as in a giant corporation. But every boss's son has a treacherous road to tread if he wants to become a man.

I stood gaping up at Hec for a matter of seconds. My mind raced. I thought: This is one of the first honest opinions I've ever heard. So what if I am Ed Wynn's son? What difference does it make? The guy on the plane is absolutely right.

He jumped down and shook my hand. He was a hero then and there. I suddenly wanted to break out of the hothouse I'd been raised in, out into the sturdy world of men.

Hec taught me that people had to work to put laundry in your bedroom drawer. He operated on the principle that so long as I went home dirty my mother would be satisfied that I was staying out of mischief. So whether the job we were tackling was dirty or clean he made sure my face, hands, and clothes were smeared with engine oil before the chauffeur arrived to collect me.

At first I expected Hec to fetch and carry for me. Everybody else did for the boss's son. But not Hec. "You want a spanner?" he'd say as we worked on the boats together that first winter. "You go get it. You want a job done? Do it yourself, and do it right."

In actual salary he didn't draw a dollar from Dad, but it was Dad who financed the fun we had, while Hec punched

With my mother in the garden of "the dusty house," Great Neck Estates, Long Island. The curls grew longer with the years. *(right)* One of my only pictures with Grandpa Leopold, who stands between Grandma Leopold and my cousin Sylvia (now Mrs. Charles Hirsch). Fräulein was the photographer.

The famed fourth birthday party. The man dressed as a child is Oscar Shaw. The birthday boy must have gone off to find himself some more ice cream.

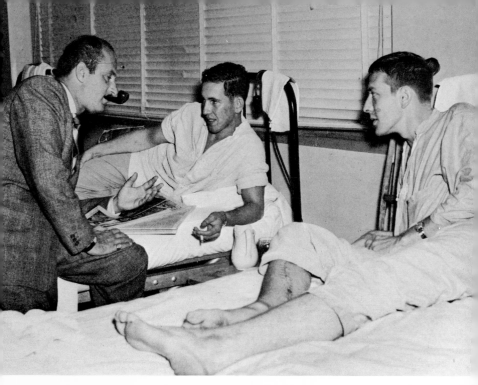

Working Travis Air Force Base hospital, California, with some early casualties flown home from the Korean War. Much less rugged than the kind of work indicated in the camp show diary.

Bob Mathias and myself on *The Troubleshooters*. Also in this series on television is, of course, Cary Loftin.

The day we won the Around-Manhattan cup. Hector, myself and his Scottie, Whisky.

Requiem cast one day before air time, when they were so afraid about Pop's performance he was almost excluded in this picture. They figured maybe somebody else would take over his part.

Fathers and sons at Skowhegan, 1938. Arthur and Buddy Byron; Ed and Keenan Wynn; John B. and Warren Hymer; Owen Davis and Owen, Jr.

Cary Loftin has some advice to give at the 1951 Big Bear hare-and-hounds ride. It did him no good. I didn't finish.

Sharley and I married on January 8, 1954, at Raney Air Force Base, Puerto Rico, by the chaplain there. Matron of honor: his wife. Best man: Bobby Tucker.

Catalina Grand Prix, 1957; second lap; golf-course crossing. The fellow in back of me passed me two laps later. That year, I never finished.

Evie and I on the boardwalk at Atlantic City, where I introduced my bride to Grandma Leopold. Either late summer of 1939 or early spring, 1940—I'm not sure which. *(right)* The Bugatti I had in 1938. A hybrid: Grand Prix body on a 2.3 litre road model. Look closely, and you'll see it still has the New York dealer's plates on.

Mount Kisco, 1940, the year my mother died. In this picture: Joe Ferrer, seated left, and myself. Blonde in a playsuit is Jan Sterling. Behind her: Clarence Derwent.

Sometime in that first summer of 1912 they posed for this one—Frank
Keenan, my mother, and Dad.

On the lawn of the Kensington house, morning of the fourth birthday party. Grandma Leopold, Dad, and myself.

home his philosophy: "Think fast, Keen. Be sharp. Stay on your toes. Use your brains."

My mother and father didn't suspect that I didn't spend all my time taking motors apart. Dad wasn't around much, anyway. My mother was content with an occasional telephone call to Hec.

She asked him early on, "What church do you go to?"

"I'm a Catholic, Mrs. Wynn."

That satisfied her. "Don't deprive Keenan of anything, but make him work," she said.

Hec was a pilot, a Royal Canadian Air Force veteran of World War I. Nothing would do but I had to have flying lessons from him. I remember one trip we took, with Hec at the controls of a two-seater, open-cockpit biplane called *The Fledgling*. From Long Island we headed for Manhattan with another plane for company. He'd made some kind of bet that we could tell the time by the clock on the tower of the Paramount Building in Times Square. The other plane had a camera aboard, to take evidence.

We buzzed Manhattan, dipping between skyscrapers, setting course along Fourth Avenue, with the skyline higher than we were. The photographs snapped from our companion plane won Hec his bet. Then they were hastily hidden in his picture album—they were enough to get a licensed pilot strung up.

There was no shortage of crazy fliers among us: Bill Gulick, for instance, who used to fly newspaper deliveries for the New York *Daily News;* he was killed at that job. George Daufkirk, who'd pilot anything with wings and a motor; he was delivering a plane when it broke up in the air. He wouldn't bail out over a school playground; when he was pulled out of the wreckage he was dying. They stretched him out on the ground, and he muttered, "Well, I'll be a son of a bitch," and that was it.

One morning Hec and I taxied a Travel Air biplane over the dust of a dirt runway at the old Holmes airport, to join in an airborne treasure hunt that Clarence Chamberlin had organized. The rules were simple. You were told which airport would be your first touchdown; you flew there, landed to pick up the next clue, then shot off again for another airport and another clue. First plane home again was the winner.

Dad drew the line at buying a plane. We had to turn to George Daufkirk, who borrowed the Travel Air from another owner. "Go on, fly the goddamn thing," George said. "The guy'll never know the difference."

Hec got us off to a fast start. We made for our first stop, North Beach, which later became La Guardia Field. In landing, our Travel Air got caught in the propeller wash of another competitor, a Bellanca. We were tossed off course, our lower left wing crumpled against an airport boundary pole. We put down in a hurry and examined the damage.

"What do you think?" I said, gingerly prodding the remains of the wing.

"Four or five hundred dollars."

"Shall I call my old man?"

"You want to get our ears chewed? We'll get it fixed."

We dismantled the wing and carted the pieces to Long Island City, to Casey Jones's aeronautical school. The proprietor gave the repair job to his students as a lesson in "shop" and as a favor to Hec. The students also refitted the wing and made good every sign of damage. The owner got his plane back none the wiser about the crash. We discovered later that the plane was "hot"; the owner was wanted for police questioning about a local bank robbery.

Calling Dad to pay the bills was routine. In spite of this new urge to be independent, I didn't hesitate about that. Dad seldom refused. It was one of the few remaining links between us. It was more than that on his part. He hoped I would forever be dependent on him; he couldn't bear to see me entirely free. He had lost my mother; he had to keep a hold on me.

The situation was made to order for me. They were feelings rather than conscious thoughts, but they amounted to this: "He needs me more than I need him. He'll have to pay for that."

Sometimes, to vary the monotony, I got Hec to make the telephone calls for handouts. It was one of our jokes.

"I don't get a chance to say much," Hec reported. "I say, 'This is Hec,' and he says, 'How much this time?' and that's all there is to it."

Hec and George Daufkirk owned an Ireland flying boat as partners, Hec having supplied the engine and propeller while George provided the rest of the plane. On weekends we worked together taking passengers on trips from Long Island beaches—two dollars for a seaplane ride, a dollar for a ride in Hec's speedboat, which I handled, the *Jackie B.*, a Belle Isle Bearcat.

I was starting to take flying lessons from Hec, so whenever we could we swapped places, George taking over the boat and me going up with Hec. On this morning, after George had just loaded the seaplane with gas, I climbed aboard, and Hec took the *Jackie B.* We had no passengers, and I was going to have a crack at flying.

George opened up the engine, and we started to skim the water. Our floats hadn't cleared the waves when a rubber fuel line snapped and sprayed gasoline all over the motor. I was too surprised to say anything except: "Hey, look at that." This kind of trouble couldn't happen to me. But the flames bursting from the engine were real enough. In seconds they'd blown back onto the control surfaces, and we were blazing like something in *The Dawn Patrol*. George's hair and eyebrows were alight.

He cut the engine, but it was too late to save the plane. We were out and over the side, putting safe distance between us and the fire. We paddled around, watching her burn.

We had to keep on paddling. Hec ran the boat straight past us toward the plane, snapped a picture with a camera he had with him, and kept snapping pictures while the roll of film lasted. Then he turned around to pick up survivors. He didn't bother about the doubts we raised concerning his ancestry and sex habits. He was in too big a hurry to get to his car and belt into town. He sold his pictures for ten dollars to the *Daily News*, which, the next morning, provided my first press clipping.

For once there was nothing that could be charged to Dad. The plane was a total wreck, not worth salvaging. None of us had suffered anything worse than a dunking, though I'd been scared enough in the finale to lose a year's growth. Hec saw his weekend business go up in smoke, but he shrugged that off. He managed to convince Dad that living dangerously was good for me; Dad didn't bother much so long as I was kept away from girls. He thought all girls were gold diggers.

Soon after the wreck we went to him with the idea of buying another boat. This one was the *Casey Jones*, a 33-footer with a 425 horsepower Liberty airplane engine to drive it. I spotted it sitting in Purdy's Shipyard at Port Washington. Its owner was Caleb Bragg, who had made a fortune in Florida real estate, and it was up for sale.

"Dad, I've seen a new boat I'd like to have. A big baby. Beautiful job."

"How much?"

"It sold for $15,000 new, but it wouldn't cost that much now."

"See what you could buy it for, Keenan, and let me know."

Hec and I went back to Purdy's. We finally bought that Garwood speedboat for $1,500. This was 1933 when most of the country was dragging through the depression. Dad, at a pinch, might have paid the full $15,000 price tag, because that year he made $600,000.

IX

Dad was a sailor who didn't know much about boats, but he loved the sea. He approved of everything connected with yachting. He liked to rig himself out in white slacks and buckskin shoes, blue blazer with brass buttons, captain's cap tilted on his head. He enjoyed going aboard with the crew lined up to salute him, and he got a big bang out of serving galley meals and drinks afloat.

He had every qualification for high-style yachting, including the means of paying for it. He never would have passed the famous standard of J. P. Morgan, that any man who worried about the cost of a yacht couldn't afford it. But then Dad could worry himself sick about anything, once he put his mind to it.

He could, nevertheless, afford $150,000 for the yacht he bought in his Fire Chief days, which was straightway given that name in honor of his show. The *Fire Chief* needed a crew of six and cost Dad $2,000 a week to run. This boat had three Wright Typhoon engines, each of 650 horsepower; they sucked in 150 gallons of gas an hour. With gas at 18 cents to the gallon, that meant $27.

The $1,500 he paid for the *Casey Jones,* which we rechristened *The Missouri Mule,* was chicken feed. Hec had big plans for what we were going to do with her, and my brain teemed with his talk.

We spent every spare minute that winter working on the boat. To Hec's specifications, we put a new engine in her and boosted her horsepower from 425 to 550. We scraped and rubbed and painted and polished. When we had finished we owned a real brute.

Hec kept up his refrain: *Be sharp*. Once he took a spark-plug wire off the *Mule's* engine while we were tied up working on her. He hit the starter, and the engine fired up, missing a beat.

"What's wrong?" I shouted.

He pointed to the number-seven cylinder, from which he'd disconnected the wire. "Pee on it." I unzipped my overalls and took aim. The electric shock nearly threw me overboard. I howled with the pain in my groin.

Hec guffawed. "Not sharp, Keeno. Uric acid's a conductor."

I was always chronically short of money in spite of Dad's being an easy touch. For one thing, the *Mule* burned thirty-two gallons of gas an hour. Then there was spending I wanted to keep dark from Dad, incurred on evening safaris into Manhattan, with or without Hec, when I sampled the stuff the rumrunners hauled and introduced myself to the art of squiring women. There was only one thing for us: we had to put the *Mule* to work. When I brought up the subject of looking for charters, Hec had been nursing the idea all along. "Let's get out and ring doorbells. You know the pitch: anything for an honest day's charter, but no crooked stuff," he said.

That's how we met the President of the United States. It was our first charter, the result of a call I made on the *Daily News*. The United States fleet was going to be reviewed by President Roosevelt some forty miles off the Long Island shore. All pictures taken by newspaper and agency photographers were to be picked up by one fast boat and returned to Manhattan for processing.

Thanks to the built-in beef of the *Mule*, Hec and I collected the assignment—an automobile test driver and a school boy. It looked simple enough. All we had to do was ride out to the fleet, accept the package of negatives, and beat it back to New York. How could you miss?

There was a detail we'd overlooked. On the morning of the job, as we set out from Duffy's, the river was blanketed in fog. Hec and I put up some combined curses.

"How're we going to find the fleet in this?" I said.

"First we've got to find our way down this river."

We crept at dead throttle down to the Bay, swung out toward the Narrows, and slowed to a standstill. The fog lay thicker than before. All we could see was choppy water, white mist, and the occasional black shapes of bigger boats.

We peered at some profiles of other vessels until we picked out the low-slung shape of a Navy destroyer poking through the soup.

"That guy must be going our way," Hec said. "Why don't we follow him?"

I dogged the gray hull for miles. Then the breeze freshened, and morning sun began burning away the fog. The sea was rising, but we'd lost too much time already. We poured on some speed to reach the far-stretching line of dark silhouettes we saw in the distance.

We found the flagship that was our contact point. We came alongside, a flea against a hippopotamus, rising and falling with the roll of the waves. While we waited for cans of film to be thrown down to us, I lay on my back on the *Mule's* bow, holding onto a line, and walking up and down the flank of the flagship with my rubber-soled sneakers. The first can of film crashed through our mahogany deck.

Under a battered hat, a familiar face peered down over the warship's rail. Franklin Delano Roosevelt removed the long cigarette holder that was clamped between his teeth. "Did you boys come all this way out in that little boat?" he asked.

I was a semi-savage youth who stood on no ceremony. I stayed on my back, walking up and down in the sneakers. "Yes, sir, and we're going back in her too."

Hec gave me the high sign that the negatives were safely stowed. I hopped back into the front cockpit, opened up the throttle, and we went full-bore in the churning sea. I waved to the President. He smiled back and saluted us, arm reaching up from under his black cape.

That season the United States around New York kept us in easy money. With a fast boat for hire, you could pick up charters for the asking. One job we collected put me into motion pictures. I made my debut as the frantic heroine of a movie called *Chained*, doubling for Joan Crawford.

Its climax saw the girl aboard a speedboat racing through New York's upper bay, in and out of the piers, missing other vessels by inches. The second-unit director was Sam Zimbalist, who had won his stripes long since as an M-G-M producer when he died in 1958 making *Ben Hur* in Italy. Neither Sam nor Joan Crawford intended to risk her neck shooting the *Chained* chase. What he wanted was a fast boat and somebody who, in long shots, could pass as Crawford. I qualified on both counts, though Zimbalist had to be convinced I could handle the job.

He arrived at Duffy's asking about charter boats. Captain Sullivan recommended the *Mule*, giving Hec and me a good rating for having strong nerves and possibly weak heads. Some units of the fleet had anchored in the Hudson the day I met Zimbalist. He was skeptical. After all, he would be in the boat along with a cameraman when they filmed the boat-ride finale. "I like the look of his boat," he said to Captain Sullivan, "but what about the kid?"

"Why not ride with him and find out?"

"Okay. Let's go for a ride and see," Zimbalist said.

He jumped down into the *Mule*. I fired the engine, and we took off down the Hudson, kicking up foam, making maybe forty-five miles an hour. I went for the anchored warships and wove among them. Zimbalist sat beside me, clutching the splash rail like grim death.

We cut in around the stern of a battleship, and I gunned the motor. We rode down the full length of the gray hull that towered over our heads a few feet away. Straight ahead, the links of a massive anchor chain dipped from her side down into the murky river. I took the *Mule* between the chain and the battleship. We went through with a foot to spare on each side of us. I couldn't top that trick, so I slowed to take a good look at the passenger.

Sam Zimbalist was sprawled on the leather cushions. On the mahogany of the splash rail I could see the dents his fingernails had dug. The *Mule* got the commission.

By now I was in full revolt against everything I'd been taught as a child. I reveled in the grease that defied soap on my hands. I rejected parents and protection, along with clean laundry. I resented the whole mixed-up business of what race I belonged to and which side of the family should have my allegiance.

I still went to Mass on Sundays because the chauffeur saw to that, but I tried to keep from thinking about anything the Mass stood for. When I dragged a razor around my jaw I still saw the dark face of a young Jew in the shaving mirror, but there was nothing I could do about my looks. What I could do was prove to the best of my ability that I had the guts to make myself a man, with the help of God and Hec.

I saw very little of Dad. Hec and I would pick up

tickets to see the *Fire Chief* shows. If we happened by in the *Mule*, we'd tie up to his yacht to mooch sandwiches and drinks. And we always forwarded the bills to him.

It seemed as though the future could be held off indefinitely. There was a wonderful sense of adjustment in me. I felt I'd started to shake off a heritage of confusion and begun to identify somebody called Keenan Wynn. My life was wrapped up in 33 feet of boat and 500 hammering horsepower. I'd no way of knowing the *Mule* hadn't long to live. In the 1938 hurricane that pounded Long Island, she was broken up against the pier to which she'd been tied, but by then I'd other interests—I was a working actor.

If those days had a climax, it was the day we won a silver cup three feet tall for lapping Manhattan Island. The inscription said: "Class K Runabouts. First Prize Won by Keenan Wynn—Hector Alexander. Time 39.55 minutes. Average Speed 43.25." This was 1934, and our record in Around Manhattan races stood unbroken until 1950.

We were set on winning at almost any price—Hec tending the engine, me at the wheel. The course took us from Duffy's down the Hudson into the Bay, then up the East River, through the Harlem River back to Duffy's. Hec had one word of warning to give.

"Watch out for ferryboats," he said. "You never know when one of those damn things is going to come plowing out just as you reach the slip. But you've got to keep going. If you cut in behind a ferry, don't cut too close or the wash will throw you."

I nodded. I hadn't any doubts. In those days, if he'd told me to make a ninety-degree turn and head the *Mule* up Forty-second Street, I'd have done it without pausing for breath.

The day came, and we took off from Duffy's fast. In not too much time there was only one boat ahead of us, and we were both hugging the stone walls of the Manhattan shore line the way race horses stay close to the rails.

Then just ahead of the lead boat a ferry nosed out of her slips, looking as big as the Alps. The other pilot didn't hesitate. Alone in his boat, he steered straight for the open water he thought stretched between the ferry's stern and the slip. He didn't see the wooden piles that had been hidden by the ferry until they loomed in front of him like a wall and it was too late to do anything about it. He smashed head on into them. We saw his boat explode like a bomb, with chunks of wood and metal hurled high over the water. The pilot, limp as a doll, was flung clear onto the piles, still clutching his shattered steering wheel.

We were close behind. I held tight to my course, feeling my stomach tighten and my throat start to close. I yelled to Hec, "What do we do?"

"Keep going. Nothing else for it."

That night, after the cup had been ceremoniously handed to us, we went on to town to celebrate. We roamed Manhattan, clutching the trophy. We carried it into barrooms and restaurants, beating off all efforts to get it out of our arms. I remember having it brimmed with beer as a kind of loving cup, which Hec and I tried to drain dry.

He had to lift me out of the cab that took us to my mother's apartment. He propped the cup and me against the wall while he pushed the doorbell. My mother let us in. It was very late.

I held out the cup we had won that day. I mumbled, "It's for you," and she accepted it from me. Then I fell dead-drunk on the floor.

X

In the thirties Dad reached the heights as a clown and the depths as a bedeviled husband and father. This was the golden, prehistoric era of clowns when musical-comedy producers thought strictly in terms of gags and belly laughs, not about ballet and plot and social significance. The customers flocked to the *Scandals* and the *Follies,* and South Pacific was a page in an atlas.

Funny men were top dogs on Broadway. The marquees carried the names of Willie Howard, Bert Lahr, Bobby Clark. Dad was bigger and probably richer than any of them. For a long decade he enjoyed what Milton Berle and Sid Caesar and Jackie Gleason came close to during their peak television seasons. He mingled with millionaires, visited with Albert Einstein, Henry Ford, Thomas Edison. He was a twenty-four-carat celebrity, a national institution.

If his brand of humor or his money could have solved his private problems, everything could have been put right in a second. But our broken-up family life was a humorless mess, and we all took it for granted that Dad's career would continue to pay off in an endless stream of thousand-dollar bills.

He had never made such money. Banks were failing by

the dozen and bread lines stretched for blocks when his comedy turned into a kind of escape for anybody with the price of admission to *The Laugh Parade* or the inclination to turn on the radio at 8:30 P.M. on Tuesdays. "I'd rather make a nation laugh than cry," he said.

Like his other productions, *The Laugh Parade* was a low-budget job held together with nothing much except Dad's talents as a professional fool. No other star or supporting player of any consequence. Just Ed Wynn and his rolling eyes and lisp and crazy inventions.

At first it looked as though he'd pushed his luck too far. He opened in Philadelphia, relying on the usual triumph plus the cherry-on-the-sundae feeling of local boy proving once more that he was better than the best.

In the front row sat Grandma Leopold, brought in from Atlantic City with some of her women's-club cronies. This was the night his celebrated "S-o-o-o-o" was born; it became a kind of label for him. My grandmother used to murmur "S-o-o-o-o" if anybody interrupted her in the middle of a thought. It was a family joke among the Leopolds. So toward the end of the show Dad threw in a "S-o-o-o-o" to give her a private laugh.

It was one of the few jokes the audience enjoyed. *The Laugh Parade* opened with a dull thud. Dad was worried sick, but he knuckled down to give the show a complete going-over. In the next seven weeks, while they toured from one town to another, he worked on a total of nineteen acts. It cost him $175,000, but that wasn't important primarily. His reputation was at stake, and he valued that above his bank balance.

Then he worked a trick Ziegfeld had taught him. He told the cast to spread the word that *The Laugh Parade* was in even worse shape than on opening night. The news spread to the Broadway ticket agents. He had one of the skinniest advance sales ever to await a musical arriving in Manhattan. If $200 had been paid into the Imperial Theatre box office, there wasn't a nickel more.

Dad wrote a check for every unsold seat for opening night and for the week after that. As soon as he got to New York he called on Percy Straus, then head of Macy's, and presented him with every first-night ticket he'd bought.

"Do me a favor, Percy," he said. "Hand these out to your employees, but say you paid for them. If you'd like to do me an additional service, ask everybody who's got one to wear a tuxedo or evening dress."

Percy Straus, a good friend of Dad's, was happy to help. Next Dad went to Charlie Baumann, of the Ludwig Baumann store, to hand out tickets and a similar request for the second night.

The Laugh Parade curtain went up on a packed theatre. The size of the turnout and the show itself surprised the critics. The reviews were good. The following day, crowds lined up at the box office to buy seats for weeks to come. On Dad's orders they were turned away. "Sorry," said the clerks, "nothing available at present."

When seats went on sale a week later there was a stampede to buy them. The Wall Street bull market was dead and buried; six million men were looking for jobs; others peddled apples on street corners. But Dad sold out his orchestra seats at $5.50 apiece and transformed a flop into a hit that ran for one hundred eleven weeks.

He always said: "Henry Ford taught me the principle of the thing." It was the trick of creating demand by cutting off supply that worked back in 1927 in the switch from Model T to Model A. From spring to December old Henry kept his factories locked and America in a state of suspense. When at last the Model A was unveiled, the showrooms were jammed from Maine to California. Dad remembered and pulled off the same effect with the staff from Macy's— though he kept Cadillacs, not Fords, in his garages.

This Model-A *Laugh Parade* featured one of his favorite props, and he always had a weakness for props. "They make a picture out of a joke" is how he explained them. In the show he devised a routine that had him playing a meek and mild waiter in a tough western saloon. A cowhand pushed in through the swing doors and ordered a name brand of whisky. After one long swig he spat it out on the floor.

"You gave me the wrong brand," he roared. "I can tell any brand of whisky blindfolded."

The waiter invited him to do just that, then tied a bandanna over the man's eyes and vanished into the wings. He came back pushing a gasoline pump. From it he served the blindfolded cowhand another drink. In Prohibition days that bit of business had men rocking in their seats and women shrieking into their pocket handkerchiefs. The cowhand took a swallow, sprayed the stuff out, and yelled: "Consarn you, that's gasoline."

Dad's eyebrows shot up. "I know," he lisped. "But *what brand?*"

One man sat through the show four times. In his box beside the stage, he turned his back on the performance as soon as the curtain rose and watched the audience exclusively. By concentrating on what he heard and not on what he might see, he had to decide whether Dad's giggle, verbal gags, and quavery voice would be enough to get people laughing when they'd no sight of the outrageous costumes, the smile, the fluttery fingers.

After his four test runs, the man in the box—George Vos, chief advertising man at the Texaco Company—decided in Dad's favor. After an agony of carpet-pacing and mental nail-chewing, he took up Texaco's invitation to star as the Fire Chief on the old Blue Network. He began at $5,000 a week, which he simply added to his take as star and part-owner of *The Laugh Parade*. He arranged to miss Tuesday-night performances so he could play on his radio show.

He suffered a chronic attack of "mike fright." He got so scared about his ability to keep an unseen audience laughing that he was the reluctant dragon of Madison Avenue when it came to signing the contract. Out of his conviction that he had to see people before he could make them laugh came one other of his inventions: he took away the glass wall that previously divided the studio audience from the performers.

The A & P Gypsies, the Happiness Boys, and the rest plugged away in soundproof rooms hung with velvet drapes and muffled with thick carpets. Dad was certain he'd die as a clown in surroundings like that. He insisted that a big audience, coming in on free passes, was essential to the Fire Chief. Without people, he said, he'd never know whether he was getting laughs or the click of switches turning to "off."

So over the protests of technicians, who saw nothing but a lot of coughing and trouble if you let six or seven hundred fans into the sanctum while red lights glowed *On the air*, the glass wall was taken out.

It was radio that converted Dad from a classical clown into a stand-up comic. It started him on a brand-new kind of career—and gave him a brand-new kind of voice. His nervousness at doing radio set his voice high. That radio voice became a mark of the new Ed Wynn, whose humor was a little more strident than before and whose fame was much greater.

The show soon picked up bigger audiences than veterans like Rudy Vallee and crept up on the kings of the business, Amos 'n' Andy, who had an edge in appearing every night, not once a week. Dad wrote every show himself, with the help of Eddie Preble, giving three or four hours a day to it and all day Sunday. This is typical of him as the Fire Chief:

"The opera tonight is very unusual. . . . The title of it is: 'When You Were Eight and I Was Nine and We Were Seventeen. It's about a boy and a girl. . . . The boy's name is J. Weatherstrip Reilley. He was born during the World War, and they called him Weatherstrip because he kept his father out of the Draft. . . . The boy has so many wrinkles in his forehead he has to screw his hat on. On his vest is dangling a golden charm—it's a piece of an omelet. . . . He says, 'What is that?' and she says, 'That is a canvas-back duck.' And he says, 'Well, take the canvas back and bring me the duck.' S-o-o-o-o . . ."

In his three years as the Fire Chief, Dad's pay check increased to $7,500 a week. The wailing siren that introduced the show became a national anthem. Dad whisked around on his sponsor's behalf, more than ever a stranger to his family.

As more money flowed in, more poured out. He had a list of dependents longer than his eleven-foot-four-and-a-half-inch pole ("for people you can't touch with a ten-foot pole"). Relatives by the dozen, who found him a soft touch; amateur and professional panhandlers; present and former employees who'd run into tight financial corners; and his son.

I saw him almost entirely in terms of the man who paid the bills. There was a flood of accounts rendered for the three lives the three Wynns lived. Hospital bills; bills for rents and taxes; school bills from Horace Mann on West 246th Street, where I went after leaving Harvey; bills for boats, cars, clothes, costumes, railroad tickets, telephones; bills for the wages of servants, nurses, secretaries.

When prosperity faded in the thirties, Dad was a symbol of Wonderful Nonsense. He created himself as a legend at the peak of hopes and happiness, when Americans saw the future in terms of dreams coming true, a chicken in every pot, a car in every garage, and sure-fire success for every man who worked for it. Now hopes had shrunk and contentment was something you remembered, but the Perfect Fool reminded his listeners of the good old days. The house might be burning, but it was still fun to picture the Fire Chief tripping over the water buckets and getting tangled in the hose.

Fame didn't change Dad very much. He was already rich and a star on Broadway when radio gave him a whirl. A citation he treasured named him in 1934 as one of the world's "ten most charming people," along with Roosevelt and Mussolini.

"I'm a nice man, really I am," Dad used to say, as if he expected an argument from anybody except my mother and me.

If I'd taken the time to look I'd have noticed the start of something that marks him today: the gentle nodding of the head. Strangers are apt to put it down to his age. It isn't that. It goes back a quarter of a century, when he brooded over his troubles and shook his head in a gesture of anxiety. The gesture set into a habit. Unless he's concentrating his thoughts on something nowadays, the head still moves as it did twenty-five years ago when he found himself in a world that wouldn't work out the way he wanted it to.

His life and mine barely touched. He was wrapped up in the "let's pretend" legend; I was starting to get hungry for reality. Dad liked to dwell in his own make-believe, where people were always kind and lived in castles built of spun sugar.

When he climbed down from his rainbows and tried to become a tycoon in business, he took a terrible beating. Less ingenuous men persuaded him that what the country needed in the dark days of the Depression was a new radio network; he could be president, they said.

So he put up money to form the Amalgamated Broadcasting System, with headquarters on Madison Avenue. The initial reports said: "The organizers expect that when the chain is complete it will comprise one hundred or more stations." One station, in New York City, was going to be renamed WYNN to honor Dad.

ABS Incorporated had big ambitions. It was going to sell programs to advertising agencies. It was out to sign a long list of sponsors, beginning with Texaco, which Ed brought in as its first client.

In the spring of 1933 he announced to the newspapers that the new chain would function within ten days. That was a rainbow-colored dream like another idea: "While sponsorship of programs will be sought, the chain is to operate with a policy of providing brief sponsors' announcements only at the beginning and end of a period, with the additional advice: 'Look in tomorrow's paper for further information.'"

Not until six months later did ABS start broadcasting. By then the brave talk of a hundred stations had dwindled and only a dozen or so had been signed. Dad had already turned away from the enterprise and gone off to Hollywood for M-G-M. The new network's debut won no more space than a few lines on inside pages of the morning papers, which carried some further information one month afterward: Dad had dealt himself out.

"I have discovered I am a showman and not a radio technical executive," he said when he resigned.

He had a new contract with Texaco in his pocket, and he was back in New York for talks at NBC. He got out of ABS only three days before the end. On October 29, 1933, the New York *Times* obituary page carried this item:

NEW RADIO CHAIN QUITS

The Amalgamated Broadcasting System, after a meeting
of its board of directors, announced yesterday that it would
cease operating as a network at midnight. . . . Mr. Wynn,
in an interview at his hotel, announced that he had withdrawn as president of the corporation not only because he
was "dissatisfied with the management" of the network, but
also because of pressure of his other interests, which demanded so much of his time.

When all the bills had been added, his former associates
told Dad the venture would cost him $305,000. He paid up,
as always.

The reckoning for his ambition to become a smart business
operator was not complete. Those fat years took so much
sheer cash from him that only the avalanche of his income
kept him solvent. The government turned up as a creditor.
The Bureau of Internal Revenue hit him with the biggest
suit ever filed against an individual.

He'd been tempted to juggle with four corporations simultaneously. Their names give a clue to his peculiar combination of whimsy and dreams of new fortunes: he called
them Sonny Keen Products Inc., Minny Lee Inc., Air-Wynn
Inc., and Wynn-Commercial Enterprises Inc. The tax laws
of the time appeared to permit their real purpose: to split
up Dad's income and cut down his tax bill.

He had some first-class company in believing that maneu-
vers with corporation law would be acceptable to the tax
collectors. John Hay Whitney was in the same kind of setup.
So were Alfred I. du Pont, Alfred P. Sloan, Jr., and Fritz
Kreisler. These names were enough to convince Dad that
what he was up to must be legal and proper.

The inspectors and, later, the Board of Tax Appeals didn't
agree. Every time Dad protested, the size of the bill in-

creased. He was cited before the Joint Congressional Committee Investigating Tax Avoidance and Evasion, one of Roosevelt's pet probes. Committee attorneys unfolded stories of Dad's companions in guile incorporating themselves, their yachts, farms, racing stables, and country mansions, all to reduce what they owed the government.

Dad's final bill from Washington came to $750,000, covering the years from 1932 to 1937. That was over and above what he had already paid. It proved to be possible to work out a compromise.

He carried off the settlement his attorneys made in the best millionaire manner. "I have heard," he told reporters at a special press conference, "that some sort of arrangement has been made. It was a matter of whether the tax should be placed against Ed Wynn personally or against certain of my corporations. The government said Ed Wynn personally, and so it appears to be."

The check he wrote was for $510,000—he still has it, framed, on his study wall. On top of that he'd run up lawyers' fees of $60,000. He had to sell his yacht to raise the money. That hurt worst of all.

XI

When I made up my mind to skip college, Dad objected. I'd no training for any kind of job, he said. And anyway, jobs couldn't be found for love or money. And what could I ever hope to be when I hadn't graduated from high school?

I told him I wanted to be an actor, and his voice got shrill. "What are you going to do? Ride a motorcycle up and down the aisles? You couldn't even get a job as a chorus boy in one of my shows—you can't do a simple dance step."

But I persisted, because at this time I had a strange sense of belonging to one side of my family. This was sudden and new, but very strong. I wanted to live up to my name and be part of the tradition Frank Keenan started and my mother continued. Grandpa Keenan had been dead five years: he collapsed making a movie at Warner Brothers and Lionel Barrymore took over. I'd known my grandfather only now and then, and I'd seen him on the stage just once—in *Peter Weston*. But in my heart I felt I was, and had to be, a Keenan, not a Wynn; had to follow my mother, not Dad.

Back in the thirties there were plenty of people who thought I got parts in plays because Dad bought them for me. They literally couldn't see me as a person; only as Ed Wynn's son, the spoiled kid that Daddy took care of. In

their eyes I was nothing, a shadow. If I accomplished anything as a bit actor, Dad got the credit for training me. If I
fell on my face, they sympathized with Ed because I was
letting him down. There was a notice, for instance, even as
late as 1940, written by that distinguished man of letters,
Mr. John O'Hara, about a flop I starred in called *The More
the Merrier*, which said: "Keenan Wynn dances with his
hands because his poppa told him to."

Dad's friends and followers—which meant almost everybody in the business—got the impression that inevitably I
wanted to trade on his name. Truth was, I'd gladly have been
anyone else in the world. He thought, when he quit arguing
against the idea, that I should be given some all-round theatrical training. So he put me into the dancing school Ned
Wayburn opened at Fifty-ninth Street and Madison Avenue
after he left Ziegfeld.

The only paid-for lessons I had in the theatre came from
Ned Wayburn's. I learned good theatrical manners, which
Dad rightly considered to be important, from Ned, who'd
been trained in the old niceties of the business, like staying
for the curtain call even though your only appearance was
in the opening scene. From Ned I also picked up what little
knowledge I have of dancing.

But it was a dramatic class, included in the six-months
course, that really appealed to me. For this I had intense
personal reasons.

Here was something you could do—play a scene, make a
speech, feel raw emotion pumping through you—that re-
lieved the pressure which built up inside. Make-believe dramatics had a lot in common with your own living. Besides,
I owed a debt to my mother to honor the Keenan name because I'd betrayed her in an unforgivable way.

It happened in the last weeks I spent at Horace Mann.
She and I were living in one of the dozen or so hotels that

were home to us. This time it was the Sherry-Netherland on Fifth Avenue, where we had a suite, which Dad paid for, and a maid, Ludy, whom Dad paid for too.

I was a member of long standing, with all dues paid, in that subterranean society, the kids who inhabit hotels with one parent or another after the marriage has gone wrong. I was a male Eloise, twenty years before Kay Thompson created her.

You played touch football in the upper corridors of the Plaza with kids like yourself that you'd bumped up against in the lobby, among the palms. You knew all the elevator men at the Berkshire, because that was where you visited your father on weekends he happened to be in town. You'd charted the route down the back stairs to the boiler rooms of the Ritz Tower.

We'd arrive at the Tower in the middle of the night when the pressures at Wyngate hit her too hard. She would rouse all the servants from their beds, order them to pack silver, linen, and blankets. Then she'd have the chauffeur drive us in to the hotel, servants and all, to move into five- and six-room suites, while I looked on, numb for sleep. We'd stay a few days, charging it all to Dad, before she could face him and Wyngate again. Back home again, the servants would put the linen into the closets and the silver into the cabinets, ready for the next time.

Now I was seventeen, and we'd switched to the Sherry-Netherland. The chauffeur took me to and from school every day. My mother was ill. She would let only her maid and me tend to her. Even I could see she was in desperate straits.

She had retreated into the cave inside herself, where she'd see none of her friends, speak to nobody much but me. She stayed in her room in a housecoat for days, hardly eating, pacing from wall to wall. She had only a spark of her faith left, and she trusted only me.

I had to let my father know. He asked me to help. "She must go to the hospital, Keenan. If she doesn't, you know, she might not live."

I nodded. "But she won't let a doctor see her."

"You'll have to persuade her to somehow. It's your responsibility. You're the only one she'll listen to. You know that."

I laid claim to no more subtlety than an ox. How could I help? What could I possibly find to say that would convince her?

"You'll have to lie if necessary, Keenan. You've got to get a doctor into her room."

I went back to the hotel. I told her our family doctor had asked if he might pay us a social call. Dad had arranged that the doctor would commit her to the hospital as soon as I let him in.

"What does he want to see me for?" she asked me suspiciously.

"Nothing, Mother. He justs wants to say hello."

She trusted me implicitly, so she agreed. When the doctor arrived, I let him in. I didn't want to know what he was doing to her, so I stayed in the living room while he went into her bedroom. He had two ambulance attendants and a stretcher waiting for his call. They carried her out strapped to the stretcher. I pressed myself into a corner as they left, just staring, sure I might never see her alive again. I couldn't speak, not even to say good-by.

I was in a frightening state after that. I had to move in with Dad at the Hotel Berkshire because I couldn't live alone. He did his utmost to understand my feelings, but I refused to talk to him. I felt like Judas, and I blamed Dad for trapping me into it. The fact that he was right and she would have died otherwise meant nothing to me. The fact that this was for her own good didn't ease my pain. All I could think of was: I lied to her and destroyed her faith in me.

It was impossible to keep up the farce of pretending to be
a schoolboy.

My mother was in Doctors Hospital for seventeen months.
I visited her every other day, but she didn't know me. I'd
sit by her bed just to be there with her, some kind of link with
the world she'd lost. In those seventeen months I changed
from a schoolboy into a man in looks and manner. I had to
grow up fast. I'd graduated from Ned Wayburn's and started
work as an actor before my mother became aware one day
that I was at her bedside.

"Who are you?" she said, not recognizing me at all.

"I'm Keenan," I said. "Your son."

"You're not Keenan. You're just pretending to be. My son
is a schoolboy. Bring him to me, please."

I started to talk and went on talking until she knew me.
It took a long time to convince her.

Graduation day at Ned Wayburn's was normally a matter
of a little dance, a little patter. I'd had a different idea.

That year at the Royale Theatre there was a play, *They
Shall Not Die*, by John Wexley, based on the trial of the
Scottsboro boys, who had been charged with raping two
white girls in Alabama. Claude Rains played the part of
Nathan G. Rubin, a Jewish attorney who goes down from
New York to defend the Negro, Haywood Patterson, who
faces the death penalty.

When I sat in the Royale one night, I tensed with emotion.
It was the last act. Rains, enormously impressive, was delivering his famous address to the jury: "I am here today for
the sake of justice . . . When the hour of our country's need
came . . . there was no question of Jew or Gentile . . ."* I

---

*This and the ensuing quotes are from *They Shall Not Die*, by John
Wexley (New York: Afred Knopf, 1934).

left my seat in a daze. I had to learn that speech. It said what I wanted to say.

For graduation the big rehearsal room at Ned Wayburn's was filled with rows of rented chairs. Dad brought a friend along, Mel Burke, who ran a summer theatre up in Skowhegan, Maine. He wanted to have an objective opinion about whether I was any good or not. His own emotions were too involved.

The other students did their dance routines. Then my turn came. Ned delivered the usual brief introduction: "And now a young fellow who's going to follow his famous father— Ed Wynn's son, Keenan. . . ." I stood up, numb.

"Your Honor, gentlemen of the jury . . . I am here today for the sake of justice . . ."

I half wished my mother were there to listen; I could feel myself taking hold of the part, the nervousness fading.

"What was the argument of the learned solicitor if not an appeal to prejudice, sectionalism, and bigotry? What he meant was: 'Come on, boys. We can lick this Jew from New York. Stick it into him.' We're among our homefolk . . . You know there have been threats against my life. Threats and warnings. But mobs mean nothing to me. Let them take me. Let them hang me. I don't care. I'm not afraid . . ."

I could feel the anger and pity of the words welling up. The few bits of technique I'd acquired in the past months weren't important. For the moment, I lived it, a noble Jewish lawyer fighting to move the hearts of his enemies. Now here it came, the climax that made your eyes itch, but offstage you could never allow yourself the pleasure of tears.

"Remember that when we, in times of need and doubt, call upon our Maker to help us, we do not call in vain. The Almighty God above does not ask if we are praying to a black man's God or to a Jewish God. No. He listens to all His children with the same compassion and generosity, and so I ask you to join with me in common prayer. (*Lift up arms and with trembling, tired voice*) 'Our Father, which art in Heaven . . . Amen!'" (*Hold a moment of silence, nod to jury and judge, return to chair, weary and exhausted.*)

I sat down blindly. The applause was there, and good to hear, but it was disassociated from me. The big, new thing was that I could escape from myself, yet at the same time pour out some of my own emotion that was locked up inside. If tears came, they were my tears, but also the pardonable tears of the lawyer Rubin or whatever future parts I could find like that.

Dad embraced me, his face streaming. "You were great, Keenan, just great. Wasn't he wonderful, Mel?"

The cheerful white-haired man beside him agreed. "Why don't you come up and join us in Skowhegan? You can learn the ropes the hard way, but it's the best way. We could pay you twenty-five dollars a week and your board as prop boy."

I jumped at it. I was certain I had all the makings of a sensational actor. Mel held back his real opinion until later, when it couldn't do any harm.

"Your great speech was lousy," he smiled. "I hired you for just one reason. Not because I was out to do your father a favor. Nor because you came cheap and looked healthy. I hired you because I knew you must have a lot of nerve to tackle what you tried to do."

My father was equally frank when I first left home to go on the stage. He made no bones about it. "You'll never make anything of yourself," he said. He didn't buy me a job, but he did get me an Actors Equity card and he bought me a box of make-up.

XII

Our family fortunes changed in 1935. I made my first dollar as a professional actor. The Texaco show went off the air, and Dad lost $7,500 a week. By his careful arithmetic, three years in radio had earned him $980,000.

Suddenly he had time on his hands: time to give to his family, but no family worth the name. Leisure had come too late. My mother was still in the hospital. I had little in common with him. He was at a loose end, and he hated it.

Of course he was still rich and still a celebrity, but idleness disturbed him. He'd have liked to make another movie, but his brand of humor didn't register in Hollywood. At Metro-Goldwyn-Mayer, *The Chief*, which had been filmed two years earlier, was one of the most colossal flops in the studio's history.

It's impossible to see how that could have been avoided. The producer assigned to *The Chief* hadn't watched Dad at work for years, and the script writer never had bought a ticket to an Ed Wynn show. The director decided Dad needed to be an altogether different kind of comedian.

Dad was dressed up as a regular fireman and made up to look like anybody in movies except himself. He was actually in Make-up when Louis B. Mayer walked in—Dad had known him for years.

"Who's that?" said Mr. Mayer, pointing to my father.

"It's Ed Wynn," the make-up men said proudly.

"Congratulations," Mr. Mayer beamed. "I'd never have recognized him."

In the thirties Dad dipped a toe into television, just as he'd been a "first" in network radio. General Sarnoff invited him to appear in an experimental telecast from NBC studios in Radio City. Under scorching lights he told his jokes and tried his gags. The picture was picked up without any trouble on top of the Empire State Building twelve blocks away.

He missed contact with people as much as he missed performing for them. He was lonely in a special way. He missed an affectionate family life, though it was difficult for him to contribute much to it that we gave him credit for, except money. We didn't always recognize his love. He'd been raised in a fond, strong family, where the mother was terribly important and joys and sorrows were shared. The emptiness he met in his own family from wife and son must have hurt badly.

It showed in his need for human contact. He had made it a practice to stand at the exit doors and shake hands with his theatre audiences. He had also reached out to touch the people who came to see his Fire Chief shows. At the end of the performance he'd hold up his hand and say, "Please stay a while. Let's be friends. I'd like to talk to you."

Then he stepped out of his role as clown into his role as human being, at which he was less successful. He talked about himself—every actor's ego forces him to do that—but he also talked about the world and what was happening in it. He never went short of subjects in 1935.

Twenty million Americans lived on relief. Mussolini had invaded Ethiopia. The Japanese were aiming for Peiping. Bruno Hauptmann had been found guilty, and Huey Long had been assassinated. In Germany the Jews had been stripped of citizenship and herded into ghettos under Hitler.

Dad always gave the same advice to his listeners: "Be kind to each other. Don't let passion divide you and drive you against your neighbor. Keep goodness in your hearts."

For my part, I'd no time to waste on the outside world. I was up to my ears in the chores of summer stock in Skowhegan. By the middle of June, Mel Burke considered I'd graduated as prop boy in his Lakewood Summer Theatre. I could take a crack at my first acting part. I was rigged out in a straw skimmer and blazer and cast as a Princeton boy in *Accent on Youth*.

Dad's Broadway friends rallied to give me moral support. He promoted a good-luck telegram for opening night with two hundred forty names on it, from Fred Allen to Leslie Howard, George M. Cohan to Tallulah Bankhead. I had to roll it up to squeeze it into my corner of the dressing room shared by all males in the cast—the telegram ran to over four feet long. I was made very much aware that I was Ed Wynn's son, a chip off the old block.

Inevitably Dad stole the show. The opening night gave the news agencies a story to put on their wires across the country; every account devoted more space to Dad than to the play and cast combined. The Associated Press reported: "Ed Wynn steamed up to Maine on his yacht to attend the opening performance and was pleased with his son's performance. Fire chiefs from half a dozen Maine cities will be on hand Tuesday night to watch the presentation of medals to Ed Wynn, making him Fire Chief of Skowhegan and Madison. He will return on his yacht to Atlantic City on Wednesday."

On his cruise up to Maine he had called at Atlantic City to take Grandma Leopold aboard. She sat with him in the orchestra seats Mel had provided, nodding and smiling at me. She had to be worked into the joke Dad told about the evening.

"Keenan's role was so small," he used to say, "that when I dropped my program and stooped to pick it up, I missed his whole thing. So I turned to my mother and whispered, 'How was he?' She gave a sigh and answered, 'His coat was torn.'"

I was immune by now to Dad's humor, particularly where I was the butt, yet I enjoyed Mel's brand, which prompted him, sometime after that opening, to send Dad an urgent telegram: KEENAN ON STAGE FOR ENTIRE PERFORMANCE FOR FIRST TIME IN CAREER. That brought Dad up on the overnight train. But this was a Mel Burke joke. I was on stage all right, but nobody saw me. I stood inside the grandfather clock which is the key prop in *Ten-Minute Alibi,* making the hands go round to fit in with the dialogue.

Mel's stable of hungry young actors had a lot of fun. There was, for example, Owen Davis, Jr., from Great Neck days, an old hand compared with most of us. One long weekend Owen and I took off to ride our motorcycles to Quebec, ninety-odd miles off. To beat the monotony of the trip, we had a few drinks and arrived reasonably loaded outside the sedate stone steps of the main entrance to the Château Frontenac.

"What are you stopping now for?" he said. "Keep going, boy!"

I rode my Harley VL74 up the steps, around the terrace that surrounds the hotel, passing the dowagers sitting there in their rockers, and out down the front steps again without stopping. After that we didn't try finding rooms at the Château; instead, we put up at some local flea bag until it was time to go back to Skowhegan again.

Mary Rogers, Will Rogers's daughter, worked with us that summer. The night her father died in an Alaskan plane crash, we watched one of those tremendous, trite sayings of theatre business come true—about the show going on whatever happens. The news arrived before the curtain went up on *Ceiling Zero*. On that sweltering August evening she went on without missing a cue, without a tear until we'd taken our curtain calls and the audience had gone home.

Humphrey Bogart worked there with us, the leading man of the company in those days before Hollywood saw him playing Duke Mantee in *The Petrified Forest* and tried from then on to type-cast him as a tough guy. So far as I was concerned, Bogie was a great teacher and a fine friend.

Sometime after Labor Day we closed the playhouse for another winter. I'd found something I'd never realized existed: companionship among men who worked with their brains. It was like the feeling of being introduced by Hec to the company of men who worked with their hands: mechanics, engineers, pilots, racing drivers. Now I had two legs instead of one to stand on, two kinds of people I could recognize as my own.

In New York that winter, while my mother remained in the hospital, I opened and closed in my first Broadway play—*Remember the Day*, which had been tried out in Skowhegan. I didn't know how to look for work as an actor, but luckily I could go back to living on and with Dad, who had moved into our old Kensington house again.

I had a good friend in Great Neck in Jimmy "Soupy" Campbell. To keep us busy and out of mischief, Dad paid us forty dollars each a week to dig out gags for him. The two of us sat day after day thumbing through old copies of *College Humor, Film Fun, Judge,* and the original version of *Life,* all of which we bought from the secondhand magazine stores on Sixth Avenue. I can remember only one gag Dad was ever able to use for all our trouble and his expense:

First man: You're so dumb you should use an encyclopedia.

Second man: I'd like to, but the pedals hurt my feet.

I made a stab at getting jobs on radio. This wasn't easy, because radio was more or less a closed shop, in the hands of an exciting group of youngish actors who handled most of the worth-while assignments. Among them was a really young and amazingly talented fireball named Orson Welles.

The only jobs I could get were the bottom-of-the-barrel scraps that better-known men wouldn't touch. At WMCA, which used to be on the roof of the Hammerstein Theatre at Fifty-first Street and Broadway, I picked up some unimportant bits on *Five-Star Final* and *True Detective*. In those days they paid five dollars for a half-hour show, which meant a full day's work, counting rehearsals. Dad paid better rates for digging gags.

The next summer I went back to the Lakewood Summer Theatre. After having not too much to do, it was good to be up to the eyebrows in work for Mel again. There was one other thing that made me happy. My mother was let out of the hospital at last, and she came up to Skowhegan to join me for the summer. Dad rented a house for the two of us and her nurse. We had a cook engaged locally, and my mother was like a girl again in her eagerness to prove the past could never have happened. We went on parties together, and we had the house filled for the parties we gave. We had a wonderful time.

As an actor I was starting to learn a little and playing some good heavies. It helped to know my mother was in the audience, enjoying what she saw. We did *Traveler's Track*, with me playing a gangster who in one scene arrives to beat up the hero.

I was consciously aiming to be like Grandpa Keenan, who had natural physical movement that made him exciting to watch. In the scene I came in the door, full of menace, and instinctively flung aside a chair to get at the man I was going to beat up. "My God," my mother told me afterward, "you were just like your grandfather. You did it exactly the way he would have done."

We were back together again, she trusted me again, and she tried painfully hard to grab hold of reality. But she needed someone close to understand her. I failed her as soon as the first test came.

When we returned to New York that September, she moved into another Park Avenue hotel, for which Dad paid. I was too busy job hunting to spend much time with her. And had a girl, a dancer, who lived in Great Neck.

Between Labor Day and Thanksgiving, I opened and closed twice on Broadway. I didn't look to Dad for any advice because I was sure he had nothing worth listening to, but I owed him some courtesy, and I served as a kind of go-between for my two parents. He pumped me for news about the plays I was doing and coaxed me into acting out bits of business I had to handle.

I showed him one scene where I had to open a door, enter with a telegram, and hand it to the mother of the household— it told her that her son had been killed. I gave it a somber reading, but Dad didn't care for that.

He jumped up from his chair and tugged the cord of his silk dressing gown tight around his middle. "Why, that's no good at all, Keenan. Fling open the door like this." He demonstrated. "Then take a fall as you come into the room. Put some molasses on the telegram so it sticks to your fingers and you can't get it off. Bump into the door when you go out." He demonstrated again. "Do you want to play messenger boys all your life?" he demanded. "Make them notice you. Let them see you're Ed Wynn's son."

I continued to go to him for handouts, but I figured I'd

paid part of the debt in advance. Not in money, but with a few dozen words said in his defense. And not so much for his sake as for my mother's, because she had been made the subject of public scandal.

Dad had been sued for $115,000. A man and wife, relations of Ed's, claimed he owed them that for taking care of my mother during her illnesses in 1929 and 1930. The story was all over the newspapers when the case came to trial in the New York Supreme Court. Each day of the hearings produced more sensational evidence, printed under fat headlines.

Dad made an angry witness. He was compelled to put up with every kind of insinuation on the part of the plaintiffs' attorney, who seemed bent on shattering the good name of both my parents. Dad was pictured as a man who had turned his back on his wife, a publicity-mad celebrity, and a chronic liar.

When the lawyer trained his sights on my mother, Dad couldn't listen to it. He got up from the witness chair in a rage. Fists clenched, he rounded on the judge.

"You've got to stop this," he stormed. "This has got to stop."

The man in the black robes was patient. "Mr. Wynn," he said gently, "you must remember that you are a defendant in this case. You cannot tell a lawyer what to do."

"But, Judge," Dad cried, "they made an awful thing of my wife." The judge waved him to his seat, and the cross-examination went on.

The case turned partly on whether Dad had ever asked the couple who faced him to keep my mother away for fear she would attack him. Dad swore that was a lie. But his word had been questioned by their attorney, who could readily fray Dad's emotions to the point where the jury didn't know what to believe. He needed a witness to back him up. His attorney chose me.

When I rode down to the courthouse on Foley Square the next morning, a gale was blowing. All through that day street signs and building cornices were ripped down by the wind. The weather matched my mood as I went on the stand.

Rain rattled against the windows as I was sworn. "Did your mother ever attack you?" It was Dad's attorney speaking.

"She did not."

"Did she ever attack or attempt to attack your father?"

"She never did."

"Did your mother spend much of her time during the periods in question at the home of the plaintiffs?"

"No, sir."

"Did the plaintiffs spend much of their time in your mother's home during this same period?"

"They called about once a week."

That was the extent of it. The opposing attorney had no questions for me. When the verdict was in we could claim a moral victory. The man who sued Dad got not a nickel from the judge. His wife was awarded $1,000. The judge had something to say: "If it were up to the court to decide, the court would have found in favor of the defendant. However, it is best to dispose of a disagreeable case once and for all."

The jurors had voted ten to two in Dad's favor throughout the afternoon, while he paced the stone corridors of the courthouse. By the time they finally reached a verdict, he had gone. He had a date at a rehearsal studio.

In bed that night I thought: "You're lucky one other question wasn't put to you. Supposing you'd been asked: 'Did your mother ever threaten her own life?' What then? Could you still have told the truth or would you have had the guts to lie?"

It was a weekend at the Plaza, one of the countless empty weekends when I came down from military school as Dad had arranged. My mother and I were staying alone on the eleventh floor, in a suite with a double bedroom with twin beds, and french doors opening onto a little balcony edged by a stone balustrade.

On that Saturday evening, after we'd been to a show, she kissed me good night and said, "Good-by." Not "Good night" but "Good-by." I was too sleepy to notice any difference. I was soon fast asleep, with traffic noise remote that high up.

In the night I woke up with a start. Everything was black and silent. I called my mother, but there was no answer. I peered across at her bed. It was empty. Then through the gaping french doors of the living room I saw her. She was standing in her nightgown on the balustrade, ready to jump.

I ran to her. Somehow, by crying or pulling at her arm, I got her down onto the balcony and back into bed. She was thirty-seven years old, and I was eleven. It was impossible then to understand any part of that night. Did she love Dad and me? Did she hate us? I couldn't tell.

She lived twelve more years after that, and when she died, she died a good Catholic, saved from the ultimate sin. In the simple meaning of the word, she did not destroy herself. She was destroyed by her inner loneliness, by her husband, and by her son.

I was the one who stayed with her that fall when we came back from Skowhegan, when she made a final effort to stay out of darkness. There was one night when she specially needed me with her. If we'd talked or played cards or just listened together to the radio, it might have been enough. She begged me to stay, but I wanted to see a girl.

I ducked out of the hotel onto Park Avenue, a young man in a hurry to kiss his date, congratulating myself on getting away. That night my mother fought her last battle with the evil things that threatened her. She had to fight alone, and she lost. She never tried again, not until she died.

So I could not avoid the guilt. Had I stayed, she might not then and there have surrendered the will to live. There was no escaping that.

Part Three

XIII

Soon after I started in as an actor I collected a nickname: *Verblunget*. That's a Yiddish word, actually a verb, meaning to get mixed up, to stumble into trouble. It was an apt description. Jim Backus or Henny, the girl he married, first tied the tag on me. It was a typical mark of the affection between us.

Jim was billed then as "James G. Backus," a slim, saturnine young man who had found as little fame as I had. "Well," Henny would say when the three of us met, "what happened to Verblunget today?"

"Oh, nothing much," Jim said, poker faced. "He went out on a motor bike. Killed three chickens. Got drunk. Broke a leg. You know, the usual thing."

We were two forty-dollar-a-week actors in a play called *Hitch Your Wagon*. We got forty dollars a week because that was Equity's minimum; we couldn't be paid less. In fact, I had two roles: as Keenan Wynn, I was Jimmy the Orderly, and as "Frank Munn" I played Speedy Malone.

I'd just broken up with the girl in Great Neck after we'd been dating steadily for two years. Off stage I was deep in the part of the lonely bachelor drowning his sorrows in the hard stuff; I was ripe for a new girl. Before I found one,

Jim Backus, who was also single then, had teamed up with me in a fun-loving friendship.

Hitch Your Wagon opened at the old Belasco Theatre in Washington, D.C., in the spring of 1937. Cherry blossoms were popping around the Tidal Basin, and the town was jammed with tourists who'd come in to see the sights. There was scarcely a hotel room to be found at any price. But Jim and I had no trouble. We lived on a credit card signed "Ed Wynn's son."

When we took a look at the dump that had been earmarked for us, I had a better idea: "Let's try the Hayes-Adams. That's a pretty good hotel. I've stayed there with the old man."

The manager at the Hayes-Adams, which houses visiting diplomats and resident dowagers, was happy to make room for us. "We have a very nice suite, Mr. Wynn. I do hope you'll find it to your taste."

The suite was a Wyngate-style setup, including a bedroom apiece with bath for Jim and me. We had a living room, dining room, and quarters for servants. I took it on the spot, without bothering to ask the price. I was in the usual state of being broke, in spite of the emergency money I could rely on Dad to send. Jim, by comparison, was rolling; he'd just had a check for three hundred dollars for recording a radio commercial.

"Has it struck you," he said blandly, after bellboys had ushered us in, "that one attraction of this layout is it comes with a sharp pencil? It needn't cost you a nickel. All you have to do is sign the tabs."

I did a lot of signing. The *Hitch Your Wagon* company lived it up. We poured their drinks; had them in to lunch; gave supper parties for them. We saw to it that they wanted for nothing from champagne and brandy to cigars. At first the management and other guests looked down their noses at theatricals slouching in and out, but Jim, swarthy and smooth-tongued, pushed the word around that he was some kind of Eastern maharaja staying incognito with a dear friend of his family, me. That cut off the complaining; in Washington's code a visiting nabob could do no wrong.

We hadn't any serious complaints even on the day of the floating crap game, which turned the suite into a shambles of sweating dice players. The game had been going on backstage. Most of the money had come out of the wallet of one man, a minor actor and bull of a man with a Tarzan's build and a rich family. As a crap shooter he was unlucky.

Roy Wilson, which is not his real name, had lost maybe a thousand dollars to his starving colleagues, who made sure of hanging onto their winnings by a practice known to afficionados as "packing in." Out of every hundred dollars you win, you send eighty home for safe keeping and play on with the remaining twenty. Roy hadn't a hope in hell of seeing all his money again.

Jim and I invited the dice players to the suite to continue the game between a matinee and an evening performance. Two elevator loads of actors, as shabby as we had to be or chose to be, were ferried up to the tenth floor.

By this time the game had acquired its own house rules. For instance, dice had to be rolled across the glass-covered top of a big table set against our living-room wall, strike that wall, and bounce back before the roll counted. Suddenly, as soon as they started playing under our roof, Roy's luck changed. Jim and his fellow villains had to dig into their back pockets, money belts, and the heels of their shoes for bills—tens, twenties, fifties—to pay Roy back.

"I know now," he was roaring. "You dirty bastards have been cheating me right along. None of you's going to leave here until I've got back every cent of my dough and more."

Nobody wanted to try. As I kept every empty glass refilled,

I heard his bellows of triumph and their groans of despair. I was happy to be host; gambling meant nothing to me.

He was making another point, yelling, "I'm going to get my money or beat the living hell out of you." The dice were in his fist when I pushed a drink at him. The dice skittered accidentally out of his grasp across the table top, and he missed his point.

The former victims were too busy grabbing at the pile of bills in front of him to notice him grabbing me. Livid with rage, he hoisted me like a sack of potatoes and rushed me to an open window. "I just want to kill him, that's all," he muttered.

I clung with both hands to the window frame, yelling. Even then nobody in the living room noticed anything wrong— we were a wild gang, and horseplay was standard. Roy was tearing at my fingers to pry them loose for the long drop when Jim caught something urgent in my hollering.

He came in with six or seven others. "We looked like pygmies fighting King Kong," he remembered later. "Every once in a while Roy shook us all off and came back at you, to try to get you going again." At last they succeeded in man-handling Wilson out the door and hauling me in again.

"Get yourself lost, but quick," Jim advised.

I lurked in the alley outside the theatre that evening until Jim signaled the coast was clear. A few minutes before curtain time I scrambled into costume and make-up, then maneuvered to keep space between Roy and myself all through the performance. "For a while there," Jim said, "I honest-to-God thought he'd strangle you on stage."

Roy had cooled when the last-act curtain fell. One thought had struck me hard during our hassle. On opening night Jim and I had been sure we'd bring the talent scouts running backstage to sign us. One scout did arrive, sure enough; he went straight past our dressing-room door with a Hollywood contract for Roy Wilson. With that physique, how could he miss?

Dad's credit was stretched once more before we left Washington. One night, after the show, a middle-aged woman of dignity and charm came to our dressing room with two girls in tow whom she introduced as her nieces.

"They're visiting from Virginia, you know," she said, "and I just happened to bring them to the theatre tonight. We all thought you gave such a wonderful performance that they just begged me to bring them around to see you. I do hope you don't think we're imposing on you."

The two young, doe-eyed creatures smiled shyly as she talked, and we swarmed around them like bees around petunias. I felt the urge to play host again. "Why don't we all have a nightcap at my hotel? Don't say no. We'd like to sit around and talk a bit."

The chaperone was persuaded. So with Jim to join me in squiring the girls, the five of us got a cab to the Hayes-Adams. In the suite we had some drinks. With our courage fortified, we made tentative passes at the girls after the chaperone excused herself; she'd just remembered she had promised to call on a friend for ten minutes. We were flattered to find the girls enjoyed the tribute we were paying to their charms.

We had a quick consultation in another room. "Man," we congratulated each other, "we're really making time with these babes."

We wooed and won them, but we hadn't much time to linger over our conquests. My girl, disturbingly cool after great heat, picked up a telephone, asked for one of the foreign embassies and a member of the diplomatic staff there.

"Mr. Johnson," she said, "this is Tina. I'm on my way over for our appointment." She powdered her nose, put on fresh lipstick.

At that moment the chaperone returned on cue. The fee, she said, would be one hundred dollars apiece; two hundred dollars in cash right now.

We two sinners excused ourselves into a spare bedroom for another conference. We didn't have more than twenty dollars between us. Then I remembered something. Dad had sometimes needed cash in a hurry. He signed a bit of paper called a cash slip that a hotel would honor if your credit was good. I called down to the front desk to have a bellboy bring up a slip immediately. The girls got paid in cash; I signed for them.

It took a telephone call to Dad to get us out of the hotel when the show moved on to Broadway: "I'm in trouble; I can't pay the bill." Our stay cost him close to two thousand dollars, not forgetting the girls.

Jim was a man Dad had to meet. He tried to keep up with all my friends, charm them, make them feel at home. What his real feelings were none of them could tell. In his good world everybody was charming to everybody, like them or not. But Dad's share of the good things in life, in particular the yacht, made it easy for me to continue as beneficent host.

I picked up Jim in a Mercedes touring car, one of the cars I owned after the Cadillac. He was rooming with Garson Kanin, paying five dollars a week to salve his conscience at being on the receiving end of hospitality. Jim and I took off for the Long Island dock where the *Seawyn* was tied up. With Dad aboard, we cast off for a day's cruising around Long Island Sound.

Maybe it was the sun or the salt air or the lift we got from being out of the city. Anyway, Jim and I were struck with spring fever. In Hec's company we'd have raced the *Mule* so close to other yachts that our wake would spray the passengers aboard them. With Jim, the day went dramatic. We stomped the *Seawyn's* decks playing Mr. Christian and Captain Bligh, with dialogue heavy on: "Some cheese, Mr. Christian?" and: "Keelhaul that man!" Out of sight below we kept up a series of shrieks: "Don't you dare touch me!" and: "Help, I'm being raped!" delivered in girlish falsetto. We dove, danced time steps on the cabin roofs, dressed up, and played pirate.

Dad endured it patiently. By five o'clock, when the Filipino steward was pouring drinks, Dad took a sip from a frosted glass and shook his head. "Now I know what you are. You're a couple of yacht comedians—very big on yachts, but you're going to find bookings are hard to get."

That May the newspapers carried one more story that marked a milestone on the downhill road of my mother and father. The date line was Reno: "Mrs. Hilda Keenan Wynn won a final divorce decree and $300 a week for her future support from Ed Wynn, radio, stage, and screen comedian in District Court here today. . . . Mrs. Wynn charged she and her husband had been separated for more than five years."

She asked the judge for permission, which was granted, to change her name back to Hilda Keenan.

The night *Hitch Your Wagon* opened in New York, a new friend, Paul Stewart, called on me at the Forty-eighth Street Theatre. He brought Tom Lewis, who is now in the advertising business, and a girl Jim Backus had known in his days as a radio announcer in Cleveland. Her name was Eve Abbott.

"Let me introduce the original Our Gal Sunday," Jim said grandly, naming a current soap-opera heroine. "Also, in one and the same person, the celebrated Skiddoo Lady," he said, naming a radio commercial she'd made.

Eve Abbott was a handsome brunette with a big smile and a strong contralto voice. "Also I've played with Katharine Cornell," she said.

"Let's all go eat," Jim said. "Where'll we go?"

Paul said, "Nothing wrong with Patsy's. We're hungry."

At Pat's bar and grill on West Forty-eighth Street you could buy a drink, a steak sandwich, and coffee and still get change out of two dollars. We crowded around a big table. I found myself next to Eve Abbott. We had a lot to talk about, though we had to shout above the din.

"You were good tonight in those bits," she said. "You could be a real actor someday. But you'd have to decide one thing first." She looked at me critically, from tousled hair to grease-blackened fingernails. "Do you want to be an actor or a bum?"

The first time I heard her ask that question, I laughed it off and talked about the cars or the boats or the motorcycles. But the question stayed in my mind, along with a sharp memory of the girl who'd asked it.

"What about that Evie?" Jim said when everybody else had left. "Great build, eh?"

"That's a bright girl," I said. "Knows what she's talking about."

XIV

A few days after our first meeting I was asking Evie for dates. I admired the strength and determination of this girl. She seemed to know exactly where she was going and how to get there, while I was floundering, trying still to break into radio, getting work in flops whose names I forget.

The bunch of young actors I mixed with were Roosevelt Democrats to a man. They were interested in hearing once and no more about my speedboat days and the other things I cherished. If I sat and listened, I discovered I could learn more than I'd ever suspected about politics.

Dad was strictly non-political, like most of the old-time stars, not including Grandpa Keenan, who had been a fire-eating campaign worker for Al Smith. But Dad scarcely recognized that politics existed, and I started out as ignorant on the subject as about almost everything else.

Paul Stewart, five years older by the calendar but fifty years older in experience, used to tell me: "First you've got to have the heart; the understanding will come from that. But don't worry—for a rich man's son, you're doing all right."

I found myself listening more and more to Evie. She could sense exactly what it would take to make me succeed as an actor. She also realized, far more clearly than I did, that

I had to start making decisions and sticking to them. So the same question came up repeatedly: "Do you want to be an actor or a bum?"

She kept on asking until I looked for the obvious answer.

"Okay, then," she said solemnly. "Let's take it from there. So you've got to look like an actor, talk like an actor, dress like an actor. You've got to shave every day and keep your hair combed. You've got to stop slopping around in dirty old clothes. You've got to stop mumbling about boats and cars and bikes like a garage mechanic."

"Mechanic" was an epithet in her vocabulary; "actor" was her highest form of praise. She tried to produce a new man. More important, she appreciated that she had to stir my own enthusiasm to the pitch where I'd work on the remodeling job harder than she did. By some kind of magic she made it seem worth doing. If I'm an effective actor today, I owe a great debt to Evie.

I didn't go back to Skowhegan for the next season. "You've always been getting back to New York too late to find a fall show," Evie diagnosed. "By the time you arrive everything's cast. Stay in New York this summer."

Thanks to her advice and the coaching I got from her and Sam Levene, I landed in a road company of *Room Service* as general understudy and assistant stage manager. This was a George Abbott show, which was important. After five weeks I was promoted to stage manager—packing the wardrobe trunks, making sure of hotel accommodations, doing walk-ons.

Now it was my responsibility to make sure every performance won the 264 laughs prescribed in the specially marked script that went with every Abbott show. Lines marked in red had to bring belly laughs; lines in blue demanded something less spectacular but hearty nevertheless; lines in green called for chuckles. If all the laughs didn't come every night, you had to call a rehearsal.

Mr. Abbott used to drop in without warning; you never knew when he'd be out front. He was also extremely firm on the subject of unauthorized callers being barred backstage. At the Copley Theatre in Boston one man kept trying to break that rule. He ignored the polite requests to leave that I made first and the order to get out that I barked at him next. I was in the middle of evicting him bodily when Mr. Abbott arrived. He was delighted to see what I was doing. I didn't know at the time that I'd just thrown a Shubert representative out of a Shubert theatre.

From whatever town we were playing each Saturday, I used to ride back to New York to spend Sunday with Evie and complain about being stuck as a stage manager instead of an actor. "So quit," she always said, "and I'll get you an audition with Guthrie McClintic." She was appearing in his *Star Wagon*, which starred Burgess Meredith and Lillian Gish at the Empire Theatre.

But I hadn't enough courage to quit until Hume Cronyn left our *Room Service* company and, instead of taking over his part as I expected, I was told to rehearse a new actor Mr. Abbott was sending up to fill the role. I stayed long enough to rehearse Whit Bissell—and we got along famously, to my great surprise—then just before Christmas 1937 I sent in my notice.

I quit to nothing. I moved into a one-room apartment in Peter Cooper Village in Manhattan and started looking for work again. Evie was responsible for my taking on the apartment, in a way. It was she who'd taught me to have some pride in myself and strike out on my own instead of moving in on Dad again. Up to then I'd always reasoned: Why not hook him? He's got money.

In January she made good on her promise. I auditioned

for Guthrie McClintic and landed the first gutsy part of my working life to that date, moving into a role that had opened up in *The Star Wagon*. So now I was in a good show, with my best girl, and it felt great. After ten weeks in town we went on the road, first stop: Philadelphia. Boarding the train at Pennsylvania Station, Mr. McClintic said to me, "You know, if you want to be, you can be a good actor." That felt wonderful.

In the summer of 1938 I went again to Skowhegan, where Hume Cronyn was my roommate, while Evie went to California on a movie bid she'd received. That was the season I played, among other things, *Blind Alley*. I was good enough as a psychopathic killer in a grindingly tough part for Mel Burke to invite Dad up to see me. As usual, I finished that performance shaking with emotion and drenched in sweat.

Dad came backstage with tears streaming down his face. "You were wonderful, Keenan, truly wonderful," he said, "but why don't you do comedy?"

I was also good enough to get a bid to go to London in the play. It could be done on a budget of $40,000, of which my share was to be $5,000. It was the time of the Neville Chamberlain peace at Munich, and money was hard to come by. I went to Dad and asked him to put up my share.

"I'm sorry," he said, "but the answer is No."

I never knew why he turned me down. I have never asked him since. All I know is that I might have been an overnight success, judging by all expectations. But I'm a better actor today than if I'd gone.

There were some more flops and a lot of radio, thanks to the new friends I had been making. I worked with Orson Welles on the Mercury Theatre of the Air. I did some Norman Corwin shows, which were among the biggest of those days, and *March of Times, Mr. District Attorney, Famous Jury Trials,* and *The Shadow.*

Then Gert Massey and Stanley Gilkey of the McClintic organization put on a musical called *One for the Money.* By my reckoning, I didn't sing or dance well enough to qualify, but Evie was emphatic: "You're going to be in it." Gert and Stanley were going to a party at the George Macreadys' Greenwich Village apartment. Evie got us invited. I stood up in the living room and acted out every suitable impression I could dredge up—the drunk, the subway rider, the man in a telephone booth, and the rest. That informal, impromptu audition put me into *One for the Money.* When I'd finished, I was so nervous I retired to the bathroom, sick as a dog.

The do-it-yourself program Evie had started me on was well under way by this time. She'd introduced me to Shakespeare: "Once you know what he's saying, it's as easy as reading the *Daily News.*" I discovered she was right. I wasn't satisfied with the physical shape I was in, so I started working out with bar bells and half an hour's exercise a day. From the way I looked and the way I felt inside, I could scarcely recognize myself sometimes.

Until I began serious work as an actor, my loves had been for my mother, for machines, and for the roughhouse comradeship of my own kind. Now something else had developed, a less complicated love for Evie. Marriage involved a problem because we held different faiths. I wasn't a good Catholic, but I went to Mass and confession. Yet religion meant mostly a certain awe and tense reverence to me. I judged I might be considered weak but not evil by the priests in needing the strength I drew from this girl.

After the show one Saturday night, we climbed into the Bugatti I was running at the time and drove straight for Warrenton, Virginia. At five o'clock on the morning of Sunday, May 11, we got a judge out of bed to marry us. My mother wasn't there, nor my dad. Neither of them knew about it. I hadn't asked for a dispensation, and we went back to New York immediately for work on Monday without telling anybody we were man and wife.

The marriage was still a secret and we were still keeping up separate apartments when I went up to Skowhegan for my fourth season at Lakewood, leaving Evie in Manhattan. I roomed with Hume again, and he was the first to hear that I had a wife. Suddenly I saw how ridiculous it was to go on with the pretense. I sat down and wrote Dad.

Where he was concerned and where I was concerned, he'd had a deep distrust of women. "Keep Keenan away from girls," he always told Hec. "Girls can get him into trouble." But as soon as he had my letter, he telephoned Evie.

"Well, I hear I've got a daughter-in-law," he said cheerfully. "I'd like to take you shopping."

He picked her up in the big Cadillac sedan he drove and took her to buy her trousseau at his expense. Then they drove up together to see me.

I was less considerate in letting my mother know. I didn't know what to say on the phone or in a letter. So I left her to get the news from reading the newspapers. It was a cruel way to handle it.

She had never lost hope that I would go back and live with her. In every apartment she lived in, she kept a room for me, furnished with the things I'd owned or wanted as a boy. There were ship models, books, pictures. There was the Around-Manhattan cup. There were mementos of school days—arrowheads I found and presented to her in empty jewel boxes with Cartier and Tiffany labels. The meals she served were the meals I liked—from prime ribs of beef with a soufflé potato and broccoli with hollandaise sauce to a favorite brand of ice cream—whether or not I was there to eat them.

Evie was shocked at first by the force of her antagonism. She begged my wife to give me up, sometimes abused her for taking away her only son. Then, reluctantly, she came to accept the two of us, and we visited her more frequently, because I felt that even company she disliked was better than none at all. She'd turn on me and grumble that I called too seldom or neglected her in some other way. Evie couldn't listen. She flew to my defense and risked my mother's contempt: "You are not welcome here, so please try not to interfere between Keenan and myself."

Evie's support didn't stop with words. On one of the evenings out that punctuated the self-improvement plan, we went with Paul Stewart and his wife Peggy to the Hawaiian restaurant opened on Broadway by Don the Beachcomber, who ran a similar place in California.

We wanted to sample the rum drinks that had made the Beachcomber's reputation and, as regular scotch drinkers, we hadn't a clue to the power of the demon rum. At two or three in the morning, when we left the bar, Paul and I were in great shape, though the two girls were sober enough.

I said, "Let's get a sandwich at Lindy's," so we set off across Broadway at Fifty-first Street. That was the year the New York cabs carried a warning buzzer to signal when they went into reverse. The four of us had just stepped off the sidewalk when a cab in a rank a few feet away started backing up without a buzz.

I was in no mood to give an inch. I banged on the back of the cab. "Watch it, Mac. We've got two ladies here."

A craggy face looked out the driver's window. "What you figure you're doing, bud?"

"Come on out and take a look."

He didn't wait to be invited twice. The hackie and I

started slugging it out in the middle of Broadway. Then another driver got out of his cab to join in, and Paul, small but wiry, took care of him.

Peg Stewart, a Boston girl, didn't like it at all. "Will you all please stop it and don't be ridiculous?" she said. Evie wasn't content with anything like that. Using her pocket-book as a club, she bopped both hackies as they came within her range. Then, eyes hot with indignation, she pushed herself between my man and me and delivered a line that became a classic in our set.

"Don't you dare hit him," she shouted. "He's Ed Wynn's son." My opponent snorted disdainfully and swung another punch.

The crowd around us broke up the brawl. "I worked up quite an appetite," Paul said. "I could use that sandwich and a beer." But I wasn't satisfied. I watched my hackie get in his cab and make a U turn to head north up Broadway. I took off running after him, aiming to drag him out and start in again.

As I reached the cab the rubber heel on one of my shoes slid in an oil patch on the street, and I went down under the car. A tire rolled over my knee. It was enough to slow me to a stop.

George Wood, Dad's manager for years, had seen the whole thing through Lindy's front windows. He came running out to help me inside with the rest of us. "I'm not finished yet," I grunted. "Get us a table by the window. I want to see that hack again."

They tell me that when I'm fighting mad I've a trick of humming to myself; in that state of mind I'm not conscious of details. Paul said later, "You sat glaring out that window, humming like a buzz saw. Nobody was sorry that hack didn't show again. From the look of you, you were out to kill him."

Dad was in Lindy's that night. He was disgusted with me. "You're always doing this kind of thing," he stormed, "picking on people, getting into fights, brawling in the streets like a common hoodlum." I simply didn't listen to him.

As it turned out, nobody got hurt but me. The nip from the tire laid me up for days in bed, and I hobbled around on crutches for a couple of weeks.

As soon as I got off the crutches, Evie and I went out again with Paul and Peggy, this time to the World's Fair that was pulling in millions at Flushing Meadows. I was grouchy as a bear coming out from hibernation, and I was spoiling for a brawl.

We elbowed our way, looking for something to eat, into one of the Fair's minor wonders called "Little Old New York," a restaurant Georgie Jessel ran. The crowds were as thick there as everywhere else. I was struggling to the head of the long line to ask about our chances of getting a table when one of the captains reached out and tapped me on the shoulder.

"All right, you," he snapped. "There's plenty of people ahead of you. Get back to the end of the line."

I felt the cold, calm sensation that comes with trouble. I measured him for size and saw he fit. I had the first punch set to go when Paul hung onto my arm.

"Keeno, please. We just got through on Broadway and Fifty-first Street. Don't get us in again. I'm too old to fight this often."

Everything was undecided for a moment, but he was right. We left peacefully. Evie had her pocketbook ready to swing again. When I needed it most she was somebody who believed in what I could do.

I often needed her belief because I seemed to have been born unlucky. The plays I got into usually looked full of promise, but they seldom amounted to anything.

Sidney Howard wanted me for his *Madam, Will You Walk?* which was a Playwrights Company production starring George M. Cohan. But the day after I visited him on his Massachusetts farm, he was crushed to death by a tractor, and without his personal touch the show never got to New York.

I had great hopes for Sam and Bella Spewack's *Out West It's Different*, but this was one Spewack play that didn't click.

I went into the new musical Gert Massey and Stanley Gilkey were doing, *Two for the Show*, along with Betty Hutton, Eve Arden, Alfred Drake, and Richard Hayden. And after the first-night performance I auditioned for Orson Welles and Burgess Meredith on the stage of the National Theatre at 2:00 A.M. They were casting *Five Kings*, and I'd have dropped a musical for a drama at a minute's notice—but Orson didn't think I was right for it.

Then in the summer of 1940 Joe Ferrer invited me up to work in stock in Mount Kisco, in the exciting company of Jan Sterling, Walter Slezak, Dan Duryea, and Clarence Derwent. Commuting to work there, I was too busy to visit my mother as often as I had been doing, though I knew she was ill again.

She phoned me repeatedly, asking me to see her, but she'd pleaded illness so often before as a weapon to pry me away for a few hours from Evie that I'd grown callous about it. I was sure she wanted to trick me again. Then our family physician, Dr. Van Esselstein, telephoned.

"Keenan, it's no pretense this time. Your mother is really very ill. She can't look after herself. You ought to get her into the hospital again."

I felt a surge of resentment. Did it always have to be me who got her to the hospital? I was still not going until Evie said, "She's a terribly sick woman. You've got to go."

When I let myself into her apartment I saw that both Essy and Evie were right. Over the years, my mother's true spirit had slowly faded; only its shell survived, a kind of devil-may-care pride. Now she was breaking up physically, so painfully ill with neuritis that even the touch of a hand agonized her.

"I know," she said, "I'll have to go to the hospital. I'll go if you'll go with me."

When I phoned Essy, he ordered an ambulance sent around, the same ambulance with the same crew that she'd ridden before. But this time she refused.

"Get your father's Cadillac," she ordered me. "You can drive, and I'll sit beside you."

I did as she asked. The two ambulance men and I carried her down to the big town car. "Murphy," she said to one of them, "you can put that overnight bag between my feet. Don't fuss with the rug—I shall be warm enough."

I let the clutch pedal up as smoothly as a chauffeur, and we set out, the ambulance trailing behind. "I don't want to go straight to the hospital, Keenan," she said. "I should like you to take me for a drive first. Go down past the Brevoort. I remember Jack Holt once took me there."

We went sedately downtown through the traffic and she looked out the window at the old hotel. "Luchow's next," she said, and when we arrived outside: "I used to bring you here to lunch when you were a little boy."

When we stopped, the ambulance halted in the rear of us, waiting until we drove on again. "Go up through the Park now to the Casino," she said. "Do you remember your grandfather used to bring you to the Park?" I nodded, not understanding just then what was in her mind.

We viewed the Casino. "I often danced there," she said approvingly. Wherever she directed, we went, Cadillac and ambulance, until we'd quartered the city. Up to Grant's Tomb. "You and I visited there together once, Keenan." To the Harkness Pavilion, where she had spent weeks at a time. To the Claremont Inn, which used to stand on a cliff overlooking the Hudson. Every place was a landmark in her memory.

I didn't know it then, but she was looking at them for the last time. She knew that.

We reached the hospital at last, and she went in with her bag, the ambulance men trailing behind like faithful retainers in the service of a dowager queen. She was forty-nine years old.

In her room there was the remembered scent of flowers, mixed in with the odors of floor wax, disinfectant, and anesthetics. The nurses could have been the same women who padded down the corridors to greet me when I came in every day on the train from Great Neck years ago.

There was time for a priest to come, but she wasn't conscious long after that. If miracles had been possible, only one might have helped: to bring back the good days when she was a whole woman, loving and loved. But prayers for miracles are hopeless prayers, and dead days can't be revived. My mother died in my arms.

The Mass was said in the Lady Chapel behind the high altar of St. Patrick's, with blue light filtering through the stained glass. It was a well-attended, sad little gathering of Catholics and Jews. Tears are universal among men. My father was there, weeping, and so was I.

The marble and granite stones of the Gate of Heaven are splattered on a steep hill not far from Harvey. In the good days, when my mother called on me at school, she had been happy in those hills. That was where I wanted her buried, and Dad agreed. She is there, the country's width away from us, but deep in our lives every day.

Out of all the things she left me—furniture, silver, jewelry, arrowheads—I valued her gold crucifix above the rest. I fastened it with a safety pin inside every jacket I wore: a remembrance, a token of love, a prayer for the remission of sin—it was all of these.

She had not been dead long when Evie, a discerning woman, said, "I don't think she would have died if she'd had something to hold onto. I think she might have lived if she'd known I was pregnant."

But that was one of the many things we never told her.

XV

The year my mother died Dad found a new revue, *Boys and Girls Together,* and came back to Broadway after nine years away. It turned out to be his swan song in this kind of show business. It was harder work now to get laughs, but two or three hours a day for weeks he rehearsed his entrance with a bunch of Indian-club swingers. They were on stage when the curtain went up, hurling twelve, eighteen, twenty-four clubs from each corner of the stage.

When the audience's attention had been fixed on them, Dad came out carrying a stepladder. With the clubs flying around, he set up the ladder in center stage, climbed it, reached out to grab one club. Then he climbed down, folded the ladder, and made his exit. This was a dangerous routine. If he faltered in his timing, a club would bounce off his skull.

Offstage, he was morose. He wrapped himself in misery. If Hilda's name came up in public, he fended off questions by quoting, unknowingly, some opinions of Frank Keenan, who had said: "An actor's life must remain private, otherwise all illusions are lost, and entertainment is made up of illusions." Or else Dad, feeling sorry for himself, would say, "People should think of a clown only as clown and even laugh at his funeral."

When we met we had nothing important to tell each other. He felt grief over my mother, but I felt both grief and guilt.

There were ways to bury those feelings. Work was a good way of forgetting. In those days radio was a godsend to any hungry actor who could cope with it. I lived on radio.

Compared with the grind television proved to be later, radio was a ball, and great training for learning to interpret a role by voice alone. All you had to care about was whether the sounds came out right. We did every big show twice a night, once for eastern stations, once for the West, with three hours to kill between shows. There was only one rule for those three hours: don't get drunk.

Without a bar rail to lean on, killing time became a special challenge. I was booked with Paul on a lot of jobs, so we killed that intermission time together. There were tricks to doing it, and we improved as we went along.

For instance, we played Nazis—this when pro-British sentiment in America had resulted in the Bundles for Britain campaign. We loitered outside the window displays of clothing that had been contributed to the cause. When anybody stopped to look in, we sneered in thick German accents, "Ach, these dummkopf British. They think they can conquer us with a lot of dirty old clothes."

Or we sat through newsreels and applauded with Teutonic glee every time the face of Der Führer appeared on the screen, until the audiences started hissing us too. We played gangster, sitting up close to a wall in some restaurant, giving the hard eye to the customers at other tables and talking loudly about bank jobs we planned to pull or rival mobsters we'd just rubbed out.

One day we shared a cab with Dore Schary, a radio writer who'd migrated to Hollywood. He joined with us in a round of "gangster" and, when he reached his hotel, backed out of the cab with his hands up: "Don't do it, boys; don't shoot me." A passing cop took us seriously. He had an itchy finger on his gun trigger while we tried to convince him it was all just for fun.

At scale pay of $87.50 a show, you couldn't get fat on one show a week. But when you took on enough jobs simultaneously, experienced hands like Frank Lovejoy, Everett Sloane, Joe Ferrer, and the rest of us could pick up a thousand dollars a week. "Only you need roller skates to do it," Joe used to say.

We played whatever script was pushed into our hands— comedy, farce, drama, melodrama. Series, serials, or one-shots. Fifteen minutes, thirty minutes, a full hour. It was great training for any serious-minded actor.

Dad had an odd kind of jealousy. I still carried his looks but my mother's personality. The stronger influence was the Keenan side. I found myself thinking as I imagined Frank Keenan would think, behaving the way he behaved. He had said, "Be as true to your art as you can; but, true or false, be effective." That made excellent sense to me.

My father resented it. Naturally enough, he wanted his son to take after himself, not make a life in the image of a dead man. He wanted Ed Wynn, not Frank Keenan, to be the dominating force; and Wynn meant being a comic. My mother had been haunted by her father's memory. She had a bench installed next to his grave in the Hollywood Cemetery, and on visits to the Coast she sat there for hours at a time. Now it looked as though the spirit of the Keenans was still dividing Dad and me. And as a working actor, I no longer looked to him even for money.

In one respect Evie was on his side. She disliked Hec. "He was good for you once," she admitted, "but you ought to stop seeing him now and all those other *mechanics*." I had no more thought of giving up Hec than of looking for a

singing role in *Life Begins at Eight-forty*. The two of us even
tried to win another cup for him to keep.

Dad owned a dark blue, twenty-eight-foot Chris-Craft,
powered, as the *Mule* had been, with a 550-horsepower
Liberty engine. Hec and I christened her *Empty Pockets*.
We decided to enter the 1940 Gold Cup races, in an un-
limited runabout class just suited for her. On the Sunday
morning of the race, Hec couldn't make it. I had to handle
her alone with a friend of his along to tend the engine.

Rain was streaming down, but a trial run perked up our
hopes; if we could race like this, nothing could lick us. Paul
Stewart drove out with Peg, Evie, and a Bell & Howell movie
camera. He was an avid movie-maker, and we wanted a
record of this day of glory.

He had borrowed a press card, and with that stuck into
his hatband, Paul could talk his way into and out of anything. When he realized he would see nothing from the
shore, he hustled himself and the two girls aboard the judges'
boat. With free drinks and sandwiches on tap, the three of
them had settled down to enjoy themselves before the race
got under way.

He had his camera on us as we poured the coal to it and
came close to the judges' boat. Just as we drew level, the
Liberty's ignition went on the fritz, and we had to cut the
engine to fix it.

The choppy water was giving Paul trouble in sighting
the camera. "Did they go by yet?" he asked Evie. She pointed
glumly at *Empty Pockets* limping along while the two of us
aboard struggled to fix the ignition. I waved grimly to the
judges' launch and went on working on the engine. We got
started again finally, but we couldn't make up the time we'd
lost. We placed second.

Paul was giving us professional coverage. He switched
lenses for close-ups of the two of us. He changed reels;

panned to take in sea, sky, and spectators; changed reels again so that every moment would be caught on film.

When the race was over, we met them at the pier. The two of us were black with engine oil and soaked to the skin. "That damn boat was going good at five o'clock this morning," I told them. "We thought we had it made. But I sure want to see the movies."

"*You* want to see them?" said Paul, dripping water from his hat. "This is a prize motion picture."

He called us when the reels had been developed and brought Peg over to our apartment for the first, ceremonial screening. But in the excitement of the Gold Cup race, with a possible assist from the judges' refreshments, he'd forgotten to take the lens cap off the camera. He had three reels of absolutely nothing.

Not long after, Hec came up with a new idea: "Let's go up to Canada and join the Eagle Squadron. Then we can get to England as fighter pilots. What do you say?"

But Evie's baby was due in the coming spring. I said, "Those days are gone, Hec. I can't do it. I'm sorry." Hec was crushed, as much as he could ever be crushed. He went to California as a ferry pilot, delivering PBYs across the Pacific. In a sense, that was the end of Hec and me. When we see each other nowadays, however, some of the old affection returns as though we'd never been separated.

I flew up to Canada on my first camp show. Hume Cronyn, a Canadian, was a good friend. Out of his own pocket he chartered a plane to take a company of entertainers up to play camp dates for the RCAF. By the time camp-show days were over for me fifteen years later, I'd flown 600,000 miles.

As an actor I was learning fast. I learned a lot more in the flops I was in than if I'd been stuck in a long-run hit. I was developing a certain full-blooded style and a reputation for being worthy of my hire. Dad couldn't understand it.

He couldn't understand why I was upset at being called "Ed Wynn's son."

Even my closest friends would say, "How's your father?" before they asked after Evie and said, "How're you?" I used to cringe when it happened. I used to listen with a kind of inner dread for the words I knew would come from anybody who knew the relationship: "Hello, how's your father?"

If you ask anybody that once or twice a day, he can take it as a kindly interest in the older man. But when every day of his life friends and strangers suffer the same strange compulsion to inquire, "How's your father?" then any man might start to feel like hammering on the walls. I certainly did. I resented it to the depths of me. I felt that I would never escape from his shadow; could never be anybody or amount to anything except the son of a man I didn't begin to understand.

On April 27, 1941, Evie gave birth to a son in the Rockefeller suite of the Harkness Pavilion in New York City. Dad was thrilled that the name of Wynn was safe for another generation. He paid all the bills. Evie respected the horror I felt at the prospect of a son being burdened with the image of his father. We decided to name him Edmond. That was acceptable to everybody. It was easy to call him Ned, which sounded close enough to keep his grandfather happy.

Another compromise had to be reached. I was born a Catholic and christened a Catholic. But I was an example of what could happen, without good will and good sense on both sides, in a marriage of mixed faiths. Somehow, I rationalized, Ned had to be spared all that conflict which could grind a child between two millstones. Edmond Wynn was christened an Episcopalian.

Two more plays—*The More the Merrier* and *Johnny on a Spot*—brought me good notices and the usual short runs. I was no nearer to a hit than I'd ever been. Meantime, in New

York, I made two movie tests, one a dramatic bit and the other a comedy, both with Evie, for Twentieth Century-Fox.

It was important for whoever watched them to see the drama first, otherwise the comedy flavor would spill over and spoil it. So Evie called Tyrone Power—they'd been together with Katharine Cornell—and he was happy to help.

He gave a dinner party for Darryl Zanuck of Twentieth Century-Fox, where Ty was a star, to show him the tests. Ty's agent, Nat Goldstone, was another guest, and he was impressed by what he saw. When Zanuck made no move, Nat went to Metro-Goldwyn-Mayer. Metro invited me out to California to test for them.

"Why not?" I said. "We've had so many flops. They'll pay for everything. Let's go." Evie liked the idea.

I did three separate character scenes during the next few days, but the studio bosses still wanted a scene with a girl. I said, "I'm not the fellow who does the romance. That's not right for me. I can't just do the 'Tennis, anyone?'"

But they insisted. The girl in the test was a contract player called Esther Williams. We played a scene together, and it was awful.

Billy Grady, who'd been supervising for M-G-M, told me, "We don't like the love scene. We don't want you."

"I could've told you. I could've played a crazy love scene, or a sick love scene, or almost any kind of love scene, except straight."

There were some consultations, and then Billy Grady announced, "You can stay at $300 a week, no more." Nat Goldstone had asked $750. In New York I'd been making $500. But I wanted a change of scene, and I liked what I'd seen on this first trip to California.

Without pausing to call Nat, I said, "I'll take it."

Except for one visit back East to do *Strip for Action*, that was the end of straight plays, at least up to the present, for me. It looked as if I could get farther away from working in a business, the theatre, where I was permanently fated to be not much more than Ed Wynn's son. I didn't know I was heading into thirteen years of almost total frustration as an actor, with the problems of having a famous father still to be solved.

XVI

I was the hero's best friend, the faithful buddy, the permanent pal. For thirteen years in pictures I played the same basic role. I was the cabdriver, press agent, newspaper reporter, soda jerk. Same plot, same dialogue; only the suits handed out from Wardrobe were different.

Anything the scripts called for, that they got. Drunks, good guys, villains, comics, straight men—I took everything that came along. In all the sixty-eight pictures I made at M-G-M, I never got the girl, but I made good money, and that was one of the things I was looking for.

Back in the forties everybody went to the movies. There were houses open twenty-four hours a day where the seats never cooled. Soldiers, war workers on the swing shift, housewives, school children, couples on a date, pensioners—they all packed in to see the dreams Hollywood printed on celluloid, preferably in gorgeous Technicolor.

No matter what was showing, the crowds came. If it was a musical, then it was the same picture in all essentials that you watched last in different colors—same cast, same story, same diet served out of a can the same way they served K-rations. If you happened to be one of the hams they wanted to slice for serving, you were sure to be kept busy.

The motion-picture business was humming like any other war factory turning out a product essential to the times. The biggest, hummingest production line was at M-G-M, Culver City. A contract player like me could make two or three pictures simultaneously, going from set to set as the shooting schedules demanded: a headwaiter here; cowhand's side-kick there; crook; cop; playboy; lush.

With a contract list running well beyond the hundred mark and stars counted in dozens, Metro-Goldwyn-Mayer still imported actors from New York. We were signed in droves—Gene Kelly, Van Johnson, Hume Cronyn, Richard Whorf. Directors wanted us around to handle the dialogue between love scenes in their pictures, the words that moved the plots along. The list of star names who had trouble getting the words out was a long, long one.

To keep the assembly line rolling, Metro, like every other studio, kept up a roster of those days in the month when its female stars weren't available. On those days we were shunted off to work with other heroines in other pictures, while the director shot around the absentee. So they called us "curse-list actors."

What you earned determined the parts you got. When a producer sat down with his director and the people from Casting to look over a script, they never figured: "That's something for Bob Walker," or "Here's a great chance for Dickie Whorf." They had their scratch-pads and gold pencils ready and calculated: "That's a $500 role," and "This is a $750 part." That's how motion pictures were cast. Then the casting director ran down his list of $500 actors and his $750 list to see who could be put into the picture at budget prices.

I fell into the category of in-between. I was never the star, and never the featured player—I was too expensive for that, thanks to the efforts of Evie, who served as unofficial agent and business manager. I was always the last actor with "and" above his name on the credits, just avoiding what is called "dog billing" in the theatre business. Dog billing dates back to the days of vaudeville, when big three-sheet posters were stuck up outside the theatres to announce the acts appearing that week. The least important acts were mentioned at the foot of the last sheet, in range of every passing dog with an urge to lift a leg. I suffered some indignities in Hollywood, but never that.

Dad, a fast man with sharp gag, was once asked by a friend, "What kind of parts does your son play?"

"Keenan Wynn," Dad answered, "is the fellow who, when Esther Williams jumps into a pool, he gets splashed."

But if I talked about my dissatisfaction, his advice was always the same: "For the sake of security, you have to put up with it. You can't afford to be independent of the kind of money you're making."

For seven years after the end of the Fire Chief, Dad had no radio show of his own. Then at last he had a new weekly series, this time selling Borden's milk. The hats, the flapping boots, the outlandish costumes were all dug out of storage. It was the mixture as before in a show that was completely his brain child.

Happy Island came straight out of Dad's daydreams of what he would like to be in the best of all possible worlds. He played "King Bubbles" in a lollipop land where refugees flocked from "Worry Park." His costume included a court outfit with leg-of-mutton sleeves and a midget crown that came from any nursery-tale picture of Old King Cole. He was back in character, as remote from reality as he could be, making $5,000 a week.

As before, he played to a studio audience, but now he went farther than that. "Television is going to be very big, you know, and we've got to be ready for it," he said. *Happy*

Island was produced with scenery and costumes and *sight* gags, like the candle burning in his ear as an alarm clock. King Bubbles had a short, happy reign, with Elsie the Cow as his leading lady.

In the days of the silents, motion-picture actors had to be exotics. Valentino drove a snow-white Dusenberg. Pola Negri led a leopard on a leash. Gloria Swanson, booking hotel space by the floor, married a string of blue bloods. This was the way to keep movie fans happy.

But by the time Evie and I had settled in, the leopards and the Dusenbergs were old hat. The studio bosses were glad we had Ned; a child was a useful commercial asset for an actor like me, because this was the era of Happy Families.

Men were being killed all around the world, and women were mourning for them. So actors were ordered to play charades in the cause of Happy Families, the idea being that we could prove Hollywood people were clean-living and public-spirited. Glamour queens were presented as contented housewives bent over kitchen stoves. Lana Turner baking apple pies, Ginger Rogers scrubbing floors, Joan Crawford hoeing her victory garden. Theda Bara wouldn't have recognized the place, but the fan magazines lapped it up.

The man of the family had to be pictured as a pillar of the P.T.A., given to nothing stronger than root beer. Our kids were photographed every time they got their noses outside the door. It's depressing to look back through the photo albums of those phony days: Dick Whorf wheeling a baby buggy; Bob Walker riding his bicycle; the Keenan Wynns with son by the swimming pool, the happy father appearing slightly mournful.

The New York actors stuck close together, doing camp shows whenever possible, taking the studios' money but not taking their jobs too seriously. How could you when the scripts came in? Occasionally something arrived with an opportunity, like *The Clock*, starring Judy Garland, Robert Walker . . . AND Keenan Wynn. Or *See Here, Private Hargrove*, where stage technique was necessary to make anything of the comedy. But ninety per cent of the time the epics were on the order of *Northwest Rangers*, where one look at the script told you all you needed to know. Or else Metro's lovable lion Leo fathered a turkey like *The Three Musketeers*.

At the studio they were always saying, "That's a typical Keenan Wynn part." I never discovered what they meant, except that I usually appeared as a vacuous friend-of-the-hero-to-whom-things-happen. When *The Three Musketeers* came up for casting, the men with the gold pencils said, "There's only one guy can play Planchet. It's a typical Keenan Wynn part."

Now Dumas took a lot of trouble to make his novels as historically accurate as possible. His Planchet is a mouse of a man, small in size, low in courage. I didn't know how to get down to his size, and I didn't care too much until I heard of another bit of M-G-M distortion that infuriated an old Dumas buff like me.

To avoid offending Catholics, whom Hollywood regards as dangerous, M-G-M was going to demote Cardinal Duc de Richelieu into a layman identified only as "Monsieur Richelieu" and thus mangle a fact of history. For once I rebelled. "I want no part of your picture," I said. "I refuse to be involved in this travesty of a book that's a classic on every library shelf."

The studio came back with the usual answer: they threatened to suspend me, which meant no work and no pay. I couldn't afford to lose the money, so I surrendered—and swore I'd get even somehow.

I made Planchet a giant. It's hard for an actor to make himself smaller, but easy for him to enlarge himself. I wore built-up shoes and a fright wig like a broken sofa with the stuffing bursting out. I was bigger than Porthos, who is supposed to be the biggest musketeer. I was bigger than all three of them.

Dad's shadow still stretched over me; going to Hollywood hadn't changed that. He lived in New York and I was three thousand miles away, but he often visited Los Angeles. When he called at M-G-M, he was big enough to bring the top man, Louis B. Mayer, out of his enormous white office to say hello. With a red carnation, malacca cane, and homburg, Dad was King Bubbles in modern dress. Mayer came out in his usual sleek gray suit, purring like a bland tiger.

Dad was affable. "Well, Mr. Mayer," he said, with everybody on the set listening, "how's the kid doing?" All the kid could do was stand absolutely still and wait for his temperature to drop.

I was never a favorite with Mr. Mayer, and he certainly didn't employ me because I was Ed Wynn's son. So I took some consolation from this evidence that he must rate me a competent actor. Or, as one studio press release put it, "a 'must' performer in musicals."

When new annual contracts had to be negotiated, Evie went to see Mayer. He and I had nothing in common, but he and Evie spoke the same language. Where I was concerned she'd become a kind of stage mother, with great ambition for me as a star.

She used to pass along reports of the talks she had in Mayer's office, pushing hard to get me promoted from hero's best friend.

"A star doesn't necessarily have to be handsome," she told him. "Look at Cagney, Spencer Tracy, Bogart. They're not strictly handsome men. I admit Keenan doesn't have the face for romantic leads. But neither do they, not by the old-time standards. Will you give him a chance at playing a lead, Mr. Mayer?"

He enjoyed hearing her out. He admired her spirit, but she couldn't convince him. "My dear," he purred one day, "you are like champagne, where so many actors' wives are like stale beer." Flattery was one of the heavy guns in his arsenal.

She did get me one of the best deals in the business for an AND performer—$2,500 a week for the usual forty-week run of studio contracts. We spent every nickel, and Evie tried for more. We were a very social couple.

Hollywood is a segregated community. The top people—producers, directors, stars—make up the "A" Group, a tag which some members aren't too modest to hang on themselves. On other rungs of the social ladder you find the lesser breeds, who can be categorized as the "B" Group.

Like all small-town society, Hollywood has its codes. In the boom years of the forties a movie première was an event similar in significance to the Horse Show at Madison Square Garden or opening night at the Met. Invited, you were in; uninvited, you were a dog. The same held true for the big parties given by top stars and producers.

The studio you worked for had a bearing on your social rating. A Paramount star outranked a Republic star, for instance, and a Metro star was top of the heap. M-G-M was the big studio. If you were an actor there, it was the equivalent of being a Harvard man, a pilot with a double row of ribbons, a Derby winner. This was true of all departments. Grips, best boys, cameramen, make-up men, electricians, wardrobe men—if you came from Metro, you were the elite. The same is true today in TV—the best come from Metro.

So Evie could push us into the "A" Group, though I wasn't a star and we had nothing like star money. But I was from

Metro, we knew a fork from a spoon, and I was Ed Wynn's son.

We mingled. When we gave a party, the "A" Group turned up. When they gave parties, we got invited. We swapped unlisted telephone numbers. At Christmas time we swallowed each other's eggnog and left presents under the right trees.

It was all very pleasant and painless. It made us a bit smug and self-satisfied, which isn't a rare human failing. I felt I belonged in this well-manicured little world, and maybe I did for the few years it lasted.

XVII

Before we got into the war I started to make camp shows a hobby of mine. They were exciting to me as an entertainer. There were people in my business who lost sight of the fact that these audiences were really civilians in a different suit who enjoyed something better than dirty jokes and naked girls. In my experience, soldiers simply liked good entertainment, and there was absolutely no need to get dirty.

When I was working in New York, I went pretty steadily with shows to places like Fort Dix and camps out on Long Island. In Hollywood I continued to do much the same thing. Then, when the war began and I started doing shows overseas, I found they were tremendously important to me. I got more out of them than I put in by way of deep-down satisfaction.

I didn't run around the block to enlist in the armed forces. I was certainly fit enough, but I was graded 3A because of having Ned, and I did camp shows as a civilian who wasn't going to be drafted immediately. I felt I was contributing something while I was waiting, and perhaps it was as important as any contribution I might have made as a G.I. dispatch rider, which is what I was probably due to become.

After a while we developed a style where we could work on a table top if necessary. We specialized in shows where we didn't need microphones, and we worked to groups of no more than two or three hundred guys. We never got up to the front lines, because no entertainers ever did, but we went as far in as anybody could and remain a civilian.

On one outstanding tour that took us over the Hump to China in the spring of 1944, I kept a diary. Paulette Goddard, William Gargan, and the accordionist Andy Arcari were out on this one. It was a typical, true camp show, where you worked anywhere, doing the best you could:

February 16. Leave Miami 7:00 A.M. The beginning of the trip is almost our end. On the way to the airport a G.I. driver of the bus nearly killed us trying to impress Paulette.

February 17. Natal, Brazil, jump-off for across-the-Atlantic flight to Africa. Gave show at 9,000 feet for fighter pilots traveling with us.

February 20. This is Aden, on Persian Gulf. Nearby is shipyard where the Ark was constructed. Boats are still built here as they were 5,000 years ago.

February 21. Karachi, India. Airport amazing—looks like La Guardia Field in New York. We are second troupe to come this far. Will get orders tonight in Delhi. Can't wait to know. Seems impossible that by this afternoon—just six days, from Wednesday to Monday—we will have covered over 15,000 miles.

February 26. At this moment we are flying over the Taj Mahal. Arrive Chabua, last stop in India before flying over the Hump. The Hump is the nightmare of Air Transport Command. Hump is the only route into China not closed by the Japs. Must fly anywhere from 19,000 feet to 30,000 feet to get over the Himalaya peaks. They've had planes shot down in daytime, so we wait for night.

February 27. The Hump! Yesterday they lost a C-46 with

twenty-one aboard. We go in a C-87 or a converted B-24. We get chutes and oxygen tubes. There is only one seat, for Paulette; the rest sit on baggage. We take off, in twenty minutes have masks on. At 22,000 feet I see lights—Jap airfield. Door blows open. Cold as hell. I move away from the door and airline pulls off my mask. Have to breathe. Ship is blacked out, but found loose end and fixed it—quick.

February 28. Kunming, China. Town built on hills. Beautiful terraced farms. Three hundred steps up to quarters. Facilities here excellent. Lived in hospital.

March 1. Kunming again. Show in hangar to about 3,500. Actually swinging from rafters. Had swing band with instruments flown in from Calcutta. Dinner with General Chennault. What a thrill! Hit it off at once.

March 4. Arrive Kweilin. On first appearance installation seems small, but the base is dispersed over a twenty-five-mile area—we have to play two a day for two days to reach all points of the field. During show, noticed tension; learned two hours later that a big raiding party from the field had been out on a mission. They all returned at 4:00 P.M. and buzzed the field. Leader was Colonel "Preacher" Welles. We hear raid highly successful.

March 5. Drove to another installation and had lunch. Mess table our stage today. It's just like a bad war movie. The pilots have nerves, get drunk, have dead eyes; the C.O. worries about his "boys." Drove to I.T.C. for evening show. Wonderful general here.

March 6. Suichwan. The airport had been heavily bombed just before we came in. So full of bomb holes, plane cannot land. We circled field for half an hour while coolies filled in the craters. When finally on ground, show started in a trench in revetment. All men were on alert. House full of guns.

Had first Chinese meal. The fighter pilots here—Texan,

Southern, New England, New York, etc.—had combined their individual styles of cooking in their endeavor to instruct the Chinese cooks in the proper way to cook "American." The results were such dishes as Yankee pot roast with bamboo shoots . . . or Manhattan clam chowder with shark fins . . . or shrimp creole with sea slugs . . . Extremely good eating just the same.

Left for Hengyang with escort of four Mustangs as we near Japs. Back that night in Kweilin for dinner with all the boys. Everyone is a major, lieutenant-colonel, or full colonel —and they're only kids. Had swell jeep ride home.

March 11. Chanyi. Played show in wonderful old walled town. Before take-off at Kunming, our unit was presented with Presidential Citation. Boarded another plane for Yunnani, a real dump. After show, left for over Hump, and weather pushed us way south. Flew into Jap patrol area and stayed there for forty-five minutes. Overcast saved us, I think. Could hear Japs jabbering over the radio about us for long time.

March 12. Chabua, India, again. A word about the "Short Snorters" Society. An autographed dollar bill is the usual sign of membership, but money is so unimportant here that most of the boys begin their snorter with a hundred-dollar bill. I had great difficulty signing these because actors so rarely see them. Tomorrow we go to Burma.

March 13. Surprise. Got off plane to find myself in Maingkwan. How we got in, I don't know. C-47 twists between trees coming in. The real front. Field was in Jap hands four days ago. Gave show on truck. Wonderful guys up here putting in lines and cleaning up remaining Japs. There was a magnetic mine near the stage here.

Saw my first dead Jap. Had my picture taken with one. Hope I get the picture. Met General Stilwell. Wonderful guy. Saw more dead Japs—one six feet two inches had arm cut off.

Told that arm is carried in retreat, cremated, and later the ashes sent home instead of the body. Fighting is about fifteen miles down road.

March 15. Arrive Loglai. This is hellhole. In swamp by river. Andy Arcari says worse than Pacific. These engineers are a tough crew. Much fighting among themselves. Had miserable tent. Rained all night. Good show, though. So to bed. Visited hospital in Tincha in morning. Left Loglai, arrived Hairy Ears at 4:00 P.M. Show big flop. Think men here too exhausted to laugh.

March 17. Ledo. A short time overseas makes you realize many things. This was our first day with sheets and pillowcases for some time. How a simple thing like this, which we take for granted, can become a luxury when you live under these conditions. If this seemed a luxury to us, it is easy to imagine what it must have meant to Paulette. She gave performances daily under conditions which seem difficult to us men, yet she was able to walk out on that truck or platform or bamboo stage looking like she had just stepped out of a bandbox.

We men often went without a shave or clean clothes. But Paulette made it a point always to look her best, thus was able to take the men out of their jungle surroundings for an hour and a half and return them to thoughts of the States and the girls they wait to see.

March 26. Tezpur. First show in rain. Got soaked so the boys would stay. Regardless of weather conditions, the boys invariably gather at least three hours before the show begins. They will sit through cloudbursts to be on hand on time. But if you as the actor should attempt to stay dry under a tarpaulin, that's all, brother! Not that we ever did. As a matter of fact, we made it a point to get wetter and muddier, if such a thing were possible, and they liked it all the more.

I always worked in G.I. clothing, but on reaching Calcutta went haywire, bought fancy British pants, bush jacket, and suede shoes. Tried to work in this outfit, failed miserably. Was no longer someone who got wet and muddy and needed a bath; I was someone who didn't know what was cooking. I had to take off the jacket and those suede shoes, kid about them, and throw them off the stage before the fellows would have any of me. As long as you share their living conditions you can understand their point of view. As soon as you get away you fail to know what they like or what they laugh at.

March 28. First mail from home and devoured it down to the return address on the envelope. If mail can mean so much to us in two months, imagine its significance to men out here for two years. I've seen soldiers trade letters, read letters to each other, go to any lengths to engineer the conversation around to the point where they can read their letters to the room at large.

March 31. Did good show at Dum-Dum and bad one at Belvedere. Too much brass around. I think shows around Calcutta or Delhi a waste of time. Should be at front. So to bed.

April 2. Palm Sunday in Calcutta. Had not been to Mass since death of my mother four years ago. However, a few weeks over here, and you find yourself returning to the religious teaching you had as a child.

April 5. Ranchi. Had crazy pilot. Awful take-off, cut engine and at last minute dropped wing. Coming in, ballooned 75 feet. Heat is terrific. Took off and flew into worst storm yet. Really sweated this one out. Was lost, with no radio contact. This storm like the one in which Wingate (Major General Ord Wingate) was killed. By following only visible road, we finally find landing strip. I got off and kissed the ground.

April 6. Ondal. Paulette on verge of hysterics from fatigue.

April 9. Each flight gets tougher. Left in B-24 for Delhi. Put Pop's name on bomb: "From Ed Wynn. Just for laughs." Our tour is just about over. After 77 performances in 42 playing days, after flying 40,000 miles, we're on our way home.

April 17. Arrive Newfoundland 8:30. Arrive La Guardia —New York, U.S.A.!—2:30 A.M.

April 18. New York. Glad I brought back addresses and phone numbers to call. Of course, the first thing that hits you when you're back is that no one knows what goes on. You think you've left the war behind. I made the first phone call. The boy is a bombardier. He had failed to mention new decorations to his family. Me with my big mouth. He thought his family would worry about his Purple Heart. On second phone call I learned that family had been notified of death of the boy I'd talked to five weeks before.

After a day of making calls I realized that outward appearances fool you. You are never away from the war. It's all around you. Every family is touched by it in one way or another. The apparent lack of concern is a cover-up for tragedy all around. All the guys I met would rather have it that way.

Camp shows became a way of life for me, something I escaped into whenever I could get off the hook at the studio. The routes we traveled covered half the world. Alaska to Aden, Greenland to British Guinea, China to the Persian Gulf. In Calcutta in 1944 I found my draft call into the U. S. Army waiting for me among the mail that had been sent on to my APO number. I showed my "Greetings" notice to the brass on the spot, and they wanted me to join up, stay on, and work under Major Mel Douglas, looking after entertainment needs in the area.

But I said, "No, thanks." I was set on going into PT boats

with the Navy. So I took the automatic six-months deferment
you were given at the end of a prolonged camp-show tour
overseas, and when I got back to Los Angeles I went to see
Commodore Gene Markey.

I talked very big about marine engines and seamanship
and navigation, to the point where Gene was persuaded that
PTs and I were meant for each other. All I had to do, he
said, was get drafted and wait for the Navy to pick me up.

But I took a ride on a motorcycle, which fouled up everything.

XVIII

When he first heard I was riding motorcycles in my teens, Dad was horrified. Not out of fear for my safety, but because he rated this a low-life sport. He had strong feelings about such things.

"I don't object when you race boats and cars," he said, "but motorcycles are different. Couldn't you take up polo if you want to do something dangerous? You can break a leg just as easily playing polo, and you'd be mixing with nicer people."

If anything, his objections fanned my enthusiasm for bikes, simply because he didn't like them. To get back to Hollywood after *Strip for Action* in 1942, I rode a Harley 61 all the way from New York. I arrived puffed up with pride, a real pavement hero.

At the studio before I went East I'd made *Somewhere I'll Find You*, which introduced me to its star, Clark Gable. The script had called for him to ride a motorcycle, and on the set one day I'd offered to teach him the fine points of handling a machine. I hadn't noticed a strong-jawed guy with a tough-as-hickory air about him who was listening in on the conversation. His name, I found out later, was Cary Loftin, and I met him again when I got back.

"I guess you know something about motorcycles," he said.
"Bet your life," I said. "Do you ride?"
"Sometimes. I'll be going out Sunday. You want to come?"
"You've got yourself a date."

I was going through a phase of imagining I was better than most of mankind, on or off a motor bike. I was from the East, so I could show the local wheels a trick or two. Sunday morning came. With Loftin, I set out with some other members of the cycle gang along the concrete of one of the highways leading toward the hills around Los Angeles. I thought their little British bikes looked chewed and battered alongside my big, elegant Harley. I wondered why the riders chose to wear leather jackets and blue jeans instead of slacks and a sports jacket like me.

Reaching the hills, Cary turned off the boulevard onto a trail through the brush that bordered the concrete. "Where you going?" I hollered. Before anybody answered I was flat on my back in the dirt. The other riders were moving along the path up toward the hilltop.

I got back on and took off after them. Ten yards or so farther along, I got off again, hard. I picked myself up and made a few more yards before the same thing happened. Cary waited until I fell my way to him.

"Anything wrong with your machine?" he asked blandly in a Mississippi drawl.

"What do you call this, an obstacle race?"

"It's just a little old ride along the firebreaks. They call it cow-trailing. You enjoying yourself?"

"I love it," I said bitterly. So I tried again and fell off again until it got monotonous. He hung back to keep pace with me.

"Why don't we swap machines for a spell?" he said.

"Anything you say."

I swung a leg over his spidery Rudge. That improved

things a little, but I took some more spills before we wheeled for home. I got back a better man than when I'd left that morning, humbled as well as bruised.

Cary Loftin was the first real friend I made in Hollywood. He started out as a motor mechanic and became one of the top stunt men in the business. From the day we switched bikes, I began taking lessons from him. He was my introduction to the Leather Crotch Set.

Los Angeles bike riders include shoe salesmen, college professors, boys from the supermarkets, and characters like me who ride partly because we caught the habit young and never lost it. There are also—distinct and separate—wild kids with gypsy earrings and pearls in their goatee beards, young thugs who fight with chains swung at each other's cheek bones.

You can ride on highways or race up the firebreaks. You can ride in the Mohave Desert, if that happens to suit your spirit. You can ride to prove you're male and independent, or because you like to drink beer out of cans and mix with your equals. You can make it as sensible as you please or you can have every cop in town chasing you.

When I started with the Leathers in 1943, movie people were rare among them, to be counted in dozens. The men who rode bikes didn't care if you were an actor or not. We did get Gable in after he'd come out on the cow trails as a spectactor once or twice.

Cary again was the tutor. The gang collected Gable one Sunday morning on his Triumph Trophy. He was fittingly dressed in heavy jeans, leather gloves, boots, crash hat. He'd no illusions about this first ride. He was taking it easy and modestly.

He made out well enough until the ride took him along a narrow path on the side of a hill. There, one of the Trophy's foot pegs hooked into the wall of the trail, and he went overboard, rolling down among the boulders. The bike landed on him.

The other bikes stopped and waited for him, but the courtesy ended there. Nobody knew if he was hurt or not, but from the hill a voice floated down to him: "What are you doing down there, Clark? The trail's up here."

For seconds he lay still, while we wondered how he'd react to this kind of treatment and not certain he'd enjoy it. Then he grinned, scrambled to his feet, and fired up the bike so he could ride on again. "Well, he made it," the same needling voice said. "He still ought to buy the sandwiches and beer."

Though Gable liked his taste of what may be the most misunderstood sport in the United States, he never got to the point of wanting to beat the world at cow-trailing. He was converted into a steady rider, content to jockey along in the middle of whatever pack he was out with, just taking it easy.

He was out on the day that Victor Fleming took a bad fall. Fleming, who directed *Gone with the Wind* and some more fine pictures, was a pioneer of motorcycling in Los Angeles. He rode when he was well into his fifties, which is a ripe old age for that business. I think he rode for the same reason I do—to hold onto the feeling of being still on the leeward side of forty.

He was twenty or thirty miles from his house, scrabbling up a steep, rutted track, when he came off and broke a collarbone. Now he had the problem of getting back along the trails which were the only road home. Gable pulled off the scarf he wore knotted around his neck and improvised a rough sling with it for Fleming, to keep the arm from moving and compounding the fracture.

"Stick around here," Gable said, "and one of us'll ride

down and get a jeep or something to carry you back. I'd gladly go, but Cary would probably make a lot better time."

Fleming grunted. "Forget it. I rode this bike up here, and I'm going to ride it down. Help me on."

Somebody steadied the motorcycle while he mounted. Somebody else fired up the engine and set the throttle for him. He pushed off, making one hand work for two. With other riders fore and aft, he came down the mountain, taking something like two hours of pounding on the broken bone, but getting there and kicking trouble in the teeth all the way.

When I grew increasingly depressed with the phoniness of most movie business, this was a wonderful compensation. At its best, motorcycling the way we did it, out among the rocks and sand and cactus, was a test of a man. It was better than racing cars or boats, because on a bike you could match yourself against all comers, not only against the handful who could buy or borrow a powerboat or a tuned-up sports car.

Anybody could pick up a bike for a few hundred dollars. It was a democratic vehicle with heroic overtones. This wasn't a sport restricted by high prices to rich men and their sons. It was what you could do with a bike that separated the men from the boys. For my kind of rebellion against authority and father images and the rest of it, this was a tailor-made sport.

From the time I came to know him, I was sure that in Cary Loftin I'd found a blood brother to Hec. The two of them were amazingly alike, one short and wiry, the other a tall, ambling guy. In any tight corner, with odds against you, you couldn't want better men at your side. Either of them would sooner die fighting than quit. When the chance came in 1957 to help Cary out of trouble, I grabbed it.

All that day some of us had been out watching a sports-car run. Carloads of spectators had driven out, thumping over trackless country to reach the site.

Now it was late afternoon, and Cary had dismounted to check some bike trouble, sitting on the grass with one leg folded under him. I was a short distance away with Lee Marvin, one of my very dear friends, who was a Marine in World War II and is another bike addict when he can get away from his *M-Squad* chores.

A car rolled down the hill toward Cary, sliding through the tall grass some feet away from him. He didn't do more than look up because the car should have gone on by. But the driver hit his brakes, the car slid out of control on the grass and slammed into Cary.

Lee and I came running. The driver was out of his car, gray-faced with shock, swaying over Cary. Cary was on his back, both legs shattered and his body twisted from the waist down. But he was stretching out his arms to clutch the other man. He hadn't breath in his lungs to talk, but the rasp in his throat made his intention clear: he was reaching out to kill his attacker if he could.

I grabbed the driver by the collar and yanked him back out of range. Cary still struggled to push himself up and clench his hands about the other man's throat. "Stay away from him," I told the driver, "or he'll strangle you. If he dies trying, he'll kill you." Lee was the only man calm enough to call for an ambulance. There was something about the driver that seemed to explain the whole sequence. I told the story to a judge months later.

Cary was a long time mending. His living as a stunt man was badly hit. His bones had been broken before—once he even rode with us with one leg in plaster to the hip, and he hid that leg in a roadside bush when a police patrol sirened us down alongside the curb on Sunset Boulevard. But after the trouble on the hillside, it was a long time before Cary could ride dirt again.

He had difficulty collecting damages from the driver who hit him. A shrewd attorney argued that the accident had happened off the public highway, and that promised a legal field day. When Cary brought suit, he needed witnesses. Lee and I went down to the courthouse to wait for the call.

At the end of the first day's wait, Cary was glum when he limped out to talk to us. On the second day Lee was called first. He told a calm, detailed story of watching Cary go under the runaway's wheels. Then it was my turn.

The setting was different from that other trial when I had to speak for my father for my mother's sake. But the day was as close as a heartbeat when I'd said my *yes sirs* and *no sirs*. The defendant's attorney was asking whether I'd seen the accident.

"Yes, sir."

Had I noticed anything unusual or at all negligent about the driver's behavior? "Yes, sir."

Could I describe what I had noticed? "Yes, sir. He was drunk."

Did I realize this could be damaging? An unfounded accusation could have serious consequences; did I know that? "Yes, sir."

Was I certain the driver was drunk? "Yes, sir."

How could I possibly tell? "I know a drunk when I see one, sir. I have been drunk myself."

The case was settled without much more fight. Cary was tired of waiting, and wasted time only added to his losses. It was settled in his favor.

My own turn had come earlier—in the spring of 1945. The delays were finished with, and I'd been accepted by the Navy. I'd passed my physical, and I had to report for duty the following day, March 11. Eleven days earlier, in Hollywood Presbyterian Hospital, Evie had given birth to our second son. We named him Tracy Keenan Wynn in honor of Spencer Tracy, whom I respected as an actor and who had treated me as a friend.

Evie was going to bring the new baby home with her by ambulance. With Van Johnson, I had ridden on the Rudge to breakfast with our friends, Johnny and Connie Maschio. I was in a hurry to get home ahead of the ambulance. Van and the Maschios followed by car, while I went ahead on the motorcycle.

On Sunset Boulevard a dog ran out alongside me, barking. I glanced down at him and pushed out a leg to keep him away. In front of me, a car suddenly swung out in a U turn, unnoticed by me. I slammed headfirst against a door handle. That was all I remembered. The rest I heard later, much later, because I came close to being beheaded. The Rudge fell across me on the road, drenching my clothes with gasoline. But my luck stayed good. There was no spark from the ignition to touch off the gas.

In the ambulance bringing her home, Evie heard the siren of another ambulance wailing as it passed in the opposite direction. I was on my way to the hospital where she'd just checked out.

The radio news bulletins said: "Keenan Wynn, son of comedian Ed Wynn, lies near death after a Los Angeles motorcycle crash." Paul Stewart heard the news and telephoned Dad long distance.

In New York, three hours ahead in time, it was evening. Dad in slippers and robe in his Park Avenue apartment was playing checkers with Earl Benham. While he threw clothes into an overnight bag, Earl called La Guardia to try for a reservation to Burbank Airport, Los Angeles.

The end of the war was two months away. All flights

were jammed, and Dad had no priority. Every time he was bounced off a flight, he telephoned Paul for news.

"He's in bad shape, Ed," was all Paul could say. "The doctors say his jaw's broken in five places. He's got back injuries, a fractured skull, and he's been cut up too. You ought to get here as soon as you can."

In Kansas City, Dad was grounded again. He stood in the terminal building telling a desk clerk why the journey was urgent when a man waiting for a plane West overheard him.

"I listened to you tell about your son," he said to Dad. "I've got a priority on the next flight. Please take it. You've given me so much pleasure on the radio. I know you want to reach your son."

Dad accepted the seat, with tears on his face. At Burbank, Paul was waiting for him with a car. But fog had shut down the airport, and planes were diverted to Palmdale, miles away. Five hours after the flight's scheduled arrival time, an airline bus pulled into Burbank. Dad was leaning out the window, looking for Paul.

"Is he dead?" he shouted.

"He's still alive, Ed. That's all anybody can say. Shall I drive you out to the hospital?"

Dad sighed. "If he's alive but unconscious, I can wait."

They went to the Garden of Allah, where Paul had booked a suite. An hour or so later, when Dad had changed his clothes and calmed himself, they came out to Hollywood Presbyterian. I hadn't opened my eyes.

Evie's nurse refused to let her leave our house. The first twenty-four hours, while I lay unconscious, three men kept watch over me—Paul Stewart, Peter Lawford, Van Johnson— and none of them was related to me or of my faith. If prayers were said, I never heard about them, and I have no memory of that night, not even dreams. I did not come to for fourteen days.

I woke in the hospital bed, remote from time and space, lost and disorientated. All that my eyes would focus on was a cheval mirror on a chest of drawers at the foot of the bed. I could make out, in the mirror, a face that looked like a devil mask. The head was swollen to twice human size. The nose was so distorted that both eyes showed on the same side of it, like a Picasso portrait in orange and green. Strangest sight of all was the chin, reaching far down on the white sheet, disjointed from the rest, with two weeks' growth of beard.

The thought came slowly: I was looking at a mask the make-up men had dreamed up for some Grade-B horror movie I would be asked to appear in. The prospect was repulsive, and I groaned.

"It won't do," I mumbled. "Nobody would believe it."

Then Dad came into the room.

Dad and his four grandchildren, January 1959. Reading in the usual order: Tracy, age fourteen; Wynnie, two; Dad, seventy-two; Hilda, four; Ned eighteen.

Frank Keenan in *Girl of the Golden West*, a famous role of his, in 1906.
Adding the boots and hat, he made himself look as tall as a tree.

Hollywood, 1925, and some kind of comment on the passage of fame. The face of the man in breeches next to Frank Keenan was once recognized around the world: Tom Mix.

Skowhegan. Owen Davis, Jr., Mary Rogers, and myself with the V. L. Harley that made the locally renowned trip to Quebec and the Château Frontenac.

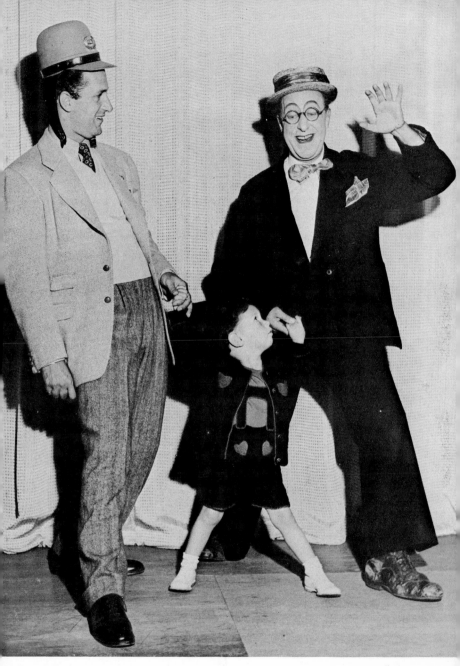

Stage debut on May 8, 1943, of Edmond Keenan Wynn, who had celebrated his second birthday eleven days earlier. Dad was starring in *Big
Time* at the Mayan Theatre, Los Angeles.

Wynn and Lewis in *The Rah! Rah! Boys*, 1902, the year Dad left home aged sixteen. This double act was booked at $200 a week.

My favorite picture of Sharley, who doesn't look this calm and sophisti-
cated when she's ushering Hilda and Wynnie upstairs to bed.

My mother and myself in the winter of 1932. She had eight more years to live.

XIX

For four months I could not open my mouth. The doctors wired the pieces of the broken lower jaw to the intact upper jaw, using one to splint the other. Diet was restricted to liquids and meat fragments chopped fine enough to be sucked through drinking straws. It was possible to talk after a fashion between my teeth, and I improved with practice. During this food-sipping convalescence, I had *Easy to Wed* to finish. *What Next, Corporal Hargrove?* was shot. Cary Loftin handled every foot of the action scenes in *Hargrove*, doubling for me.

"Hell, Keeno," he said when the picture was finished, "there's more of me in this than you."

The crash had two permanent results. The doctors refused to clear me for service in the Navy or any other branch of the forces. And marriage with Evie lasted two years longer than we'd expected.

It had been going wrong for a long time. In the beginning it had been good for both of us, probably better for me than for her, because I needed her determination to get started working seriously as an actor. What we had in common was somebody called Keenan Wynn. Suddenly, soon after we arrived in Hollywood, we had nothing in com-

mon, no shared interests except our son Ned. I had run into
a cul-de-sac at M-G-M, and that was bad for all of us.

Our marriage had followed the inevitable, sad course of
marriages in decline. We had gone from coolness to bicker-
ing and then to open disputes, sometimes in Ned's hearing.
It was plain to us both that nothing was better designed to
turn him into a nervous wreck, which was something to
avoid at any cost. Our plans for separation were well along
when the stray dog ran into the bike.

My debt to Evie was extended. She stuck with me when
I was hurt, and she stood by me during the following months
when I came very close to throwing away everything I had
hoped to accomplish. We were a sorry pair that spring. While
I was kept in the hospital, the nurse Evie had hired for
the new baby walked out on her. Evie herself had to stay
in bed with a lingering hip infection caused by shots of a
recently discovered wonder drug called penicillin that doctors
were not too familiar with in 1945.

Paul and Peg Stewart rescued us. They moved into our
house to take charge of our affairs. Paul looked out for Ned,
who had a joyless fourth birthday; Peggy nursed Evie and
cared for Tracy. Dad had gone back to New York.

It was there, later, that he shook his head and told some
friends about the confusion he had found in our lives: "I
can't keep them straight. Evie loves Keenan. Keenan loves
Evie. Van loves Evie. Evie loves Van. Van loves Keenan.
Keenan loves Van."

Van Johnson was one of my good friends and the man
Evie wanted to marry.

The three of us had met in New York when he landed a
spot in Leonard Sillman's *New Faces,* making maybe thirty
dollars a week as a dancer. Nobody could dislike this husky
hunk of freckled health, and we liked him very much. Compared with Van, most of us were worldly sophisticates.

Paul and I, for instance, kept up a running gag of scurrying around to the stage door of the Shubert Theatre every night to catch Katharine Hepburn leave after starring in *The Philadelphia Story*. We mingled with the idiot fans and yelled, "Yoo hoo, Miss Hepburn! Smile for us, please, Miss Hepburn!" Van, by contrast, used to stand with the kids that haunted the Twenty-one and watch them beg for autographs as the celebrities of the day made their careful exits and entrances.

When George Abbott started casting John O'Hara's *Pal Joey*, Van was back in the chorus again, but he was handed more jobs every day. He proved he could make June Havoc a good dance partner. He promoted himself a ten-line speaking part.

Like so many people involved in *Joey*, Van finally got a Hollywood offer. He signed with Warner Brothers at $300 a week. After he arrived on the Coast, there was nothing for him to do, so he bought himself a car and, in between sitting on the beach and driving the new convertible, he kept in touch with Gene Kelly, who played the lead in *Joey* and was now under contract to David Selznick.

Gene was one of the group from New York that stuck together, so Evie and I met Van again. After one nothing picture for Warners, they let him go, but not before he'd been introduced to Lillian Burns, the dramatic coach at Metro. Three days and one screen test later, he had signed an M-G-M contract. We were working in the same back yard, and our friendship really got into gear.

He bought a Harley like the bike on which I'd met Cary. Van came out on Sunday rides, plugging along, enjoying himself, and leaving the hell-for-leather stuff to hotter heads than his.

One day when we were out riding the firebreaks—this was before my crash—I was rearing to go but holding the speed

down, because he was still new to this cow-trailing kick.
Over one hill we sighted another bunch of riders. I temporarily forgot about him and set off hell-bent down the grade,
to roar through the other cluster of bikes and up another
rise ahead.

Somewhere short of the crest of that second hill, I hit a
rock and arched over the handle bars. Sprawling on the
ground, winded, I saw Van coming after me, sitting bolt
upright on a machine that, according to every law of the
business, must fail to make the climb. But he chugged
steadily up and waved to me as he rode by.

Some Sunday mornings we set out at five-thirty to reach
meets a hundred miles away. We took a car, with the bikes
roped tight in a two-wheel trailer hitched behind us. We
packed sandwiches and beer to drink on the way. We rode
hard and came home battered but glowing with that wonderful refreshment of spirit I found motorcycling to be.

Or sometimes, like kids playing hooky, we went out to
amusement parks and rode the roller coasters, having a great,
anonymous time. This was before Van's career took off like
a jet and he started raising a public panic.

In the first movie for M-G-M he was disguised with black
hair dye and crepe hair to play a bit in one of the *Crime Does
Not Pay* series. Nothing happened. Then he was handed a
small part in *The War against Mrs. Hadley*, where the red
hair and freckles had a chance to show, and he began to
roll. In a matter of two years only Bing Crosby was bigger
box office than Van, who had turned out to be the most
valuable property on the M-G-M list. Before he reached
that high, he came close to dying in a car crash with Evie
and me.

The three of us kept steady company, with Van, a bachelor, squiring a variety of dates to make up the foursome.
When I was away on camp shows I asked him to escort

Evie as part of the natural order of things. The studio had
scented the sweet smell of box-office dollars that was sur-
rounding Van when they cast him to support Spencer Tracy
and Irene Dunne in *A Guy Named Joe*, which Victor Fleming was going to direct. This was big promotion.

One night, Van in his convertible was driving Evie,
myself, and two servicemen friends of ours out to Culver
City, where a Spencer Tracy-Katharine Hepburn picture,
Keeper of the Flame, was going to be run off for Van's
benefit as a preliminary to his working in the new movie.
Another car ran through a red light smack into the side of
Van's convertible and sent it rolling on its side. The other
driver escaped unharmed. The four of us were badly shaken,
nothing more. But Van clung to his steering wheel, and his
head was smashed against the top lock of his car in the
middle of the windshield frame.

"I told myself, *Here goes everything*," he said later to
Pete Martin, who wrote an article about it. "My face was
wet, and I thought it was raining, but it was blood. I lost
quarts of blood—more than anybody can lose and live, I've
been told. I had been to the blood bank every eight weeks
. . . and I remember thinking, *I could use some of that stuff
now*.

"One ambulance came clanging up, but its crew decided
they couldn't take me in, because I was just outside of their
territory. Finally, the right ambulance arrived and rushed
me to the hospital. My nose was up against my eyes, and
my scalp had come unstuck. They lifted it up like a flap and
poured in handfuls of sulfa. Then they took a section of
bone out of my arm and put it into my head. I kept thinking,
I haven't got time to be sick; I've got a picture to make."*

That night I stayed at the hospital, keeping a watch for
Van and putting up some prayers for him. The doctors were

*From *The Saturday Evening Post*, June 30, 1945. "Bobby-Sox Blitzer," by
Pete Martin.

saying, "He'll never work in movies again. He'll be lucky if he lives through this."

As soon as he had gone through his first big operation and regained consciousness again, Victor Fleming and Spencer Tracy came in to talk. "We won't start the picture without you," they promised Van. "We'll wait until you're well again."

Four months later, after a great battle for recovery, Van reported in to make *A Guy Named Joe*. Two years after that he sat with Paul Stewart and Peter Lawford in another hospital room to help get me through a night when death moved in close.

By then he had achieved something that almost never happens except in fan magazines. When his convalescence was over, two pictures in which he had good parts were released within a month of each other. Without any studio build-up, with no special plugs in newspapers or magazines or on public-appearance tours, Van Johnson was an honest-to-goodness motion-picture star.

Our trips to ride the roller coasters were finished. The fans mobbed him on sight. Youngsters climbed over fences and crawled under cars to get at him. They ripped his clothes and tore off coat buttons. He'd come out of these encounters with lipstick smearing his face. It was as much as his life was worth to arrive at a movie première, and the studio was afraid to let him make personal appearances anywhere.

The Sunday-morning bike rides continued for a while as one of the rare outings he could take. But after my crack-up he saw writing on the wall and got rid of his bike, like some other Sunday riders. It didn't cut down on our friendship. We made a lot of pictures together, from *No Leave, No Love* to *Men of the Fighting Lady*. The two of us continued to go around together with Evie.

Some of his appeal to the bobby-sox brigade had to be due to his remaining a bachelor. A lot of his fan mail came along the line of: "Don't get married yet; wait for me to grow up." The angle the studio publicity team developed for him in interviews was: "Perhaps I'll marry after I'm thirty; I'm too busy right now."

He told one interviewer, according to script, "I don't think I'll marry an actress. One actor in the family is enough. The only positive qualifications for the girl I'd like to marry are: She should be an active dame who plays tennis and rides horseback and has a sense of humor. She must like to dance, but beauty is not essential." The fact was, he wanted to marry Evie, and I wanted to do whatever she wanted most, provided Ned was not badly hurt.

The tensions in the situation built up violence inside. Not violence directed against either of them, because the three of us saw the inevitability of what was happening, but violence exploding outward indiscriminately. I came home from the hospital full of tension.

We gave a party to celebrate V-J Day. The details of the night are hard to remember through the gauze of many drinks, taken contrary to doctors' orders. But one of the guests had brought along a man I suddenly disliked. I sat watching him, waiting for a moment to pick a fight.

Paul was worried. He'd been keeping an eye on me. He tried to reason: "Take it easy, will you? You're in no condition to pick on anybody. You know what the doctors told you—get smacked on the jaw again and they can't fix you up." It made no difference to what I intended to do.

Now Paul was whispering to other friends, "If Keeno gets slugged on the chin, it's the end. His face will be gone to hell for keeps, and he'll never be able to talk again." It still made no difference.

The time came, and I went over to the man, who qualified

in size and weight. On some pretext I invited him outside to fight. He was willing. We started to swing at each other. Who gave a damn about a busted jaw?

Paul came running out the door with Peter Lawford and Johnny Maschio, who used to be a prize fighter. I kept on punching. It took the three of them to stop us. Finally Maschio locked his arms around me in a wrestler's hold, and I was too much out of training to do anything about that. They got us inside the house again. I still churned with anger.

I raved, "Let me go. I'm going to kill him." In the end, I think I fell asleep.

We wanted a little dignity about the end of our marriage, but it wasn't to be that way. The studio would have preferred a different ending, too. Mr. Mayer was scared about bad publicity for Van and fretted over the effect at the box office when the bobby-soxers' bachelor became a married man.

Dad continued to shake his head. He complained to a friend, "I still can't get it straight. Tonight Keenan and Evie are out together. Tomorrow he's going to put her on a train for Sun Valley to get a divorce."

There were a lot of train rides and a lot of headlines while the details of what we were going to do were settled as painlessly as possible. Ned and Tracy had to be taken care of, which meant that money had to be provided for them. Money was never anything of tremendous importance to me, so we had no arguments there.

But Dad, who had made a fortune in hard work and not much happiness, took money seriously. He was outraged by the settlement Evie and I came to.

"All the millionaires I have known were never so idiotic as you," he said. "Harriman, the railroad magnate who held you on his knee when you were a child, didn't give away his railroads to any woman. You are giving away your house, your furniture, your shirt studs and cuff links. And to whom? To your wife and your best friend!"

It didn't matter. If they were happy and our sons were looked after, I had no complaints to make. In the end I gave away almost everything, which seemed an appropriate gesture to make. The grand piano that had been my mother's; the handsome furniture and the jewelry that had been hers too; most of her silver, the pictures, and the other things we'd shipped from New York after her death. There were some pangs in this parting, but I imagined I'd get over them. I kept my books and my phonograph records, which was good enough for me.

Ned and Tracy were saved from most of the scars that come when parents haggle. Divorce laws treat children as chattels to be awarded to one side or the other, so some formal words on paper had to be concocted. But essentially Evie and I continued to share them, though ostensibly they were to live with her.

When the last details had been ironed out, Evie and Van flew in a chartered plane to El Paso, to cross the border there to Juarez. Our two sons stayed with me. In her handbag she carried my power of attorney so that she could obtain a divorce by proxy and remarry in a single day.

Ned and Tracy stayed with me and our nurse, Maria, while Evie and Van were on their honeymoon. There remained only the job of letting Ned know about the change. I had a way for making sure he was spared any tearful scenes. He got the news in the most objective way I could devise. He accepted the fact that his mother and father were divorced because I carefully, casually turned on a radio newscast that had the story. He took it well.

This was something else Dad couldn't understand.

XX

Another Christmas had arrived, and this year I had not been looking forward to it. Unless you could build a holiday in your heart, Christmas in southern California was a peculiar holiday at best to anyone used to different scenes and climates. Poinsettias were a poor substitute for holly; smog didn't compare well with snow; the carols booming over loud-speakers outside churches and supermarkets had a hollow ring in my ears.

Evie and Van had found a new house, where Ned and Tracy lived with them, while I stayed on at our old address, now much too big and empty for me. For company I had Adolph, a German houseman, and he had helped dress up the house for the holiday. I had bought a tree that reached to the ceiling, and we had to cut back its top before we could squeeze on the Star. We had strung it with lights and hung it with ornaments, draped it with tinsel and foot-long icicles.

It stood in the living room, as handsome a tree as you could wish for. I set to remembering other Christmases when we honored the birthday of Our Lord.

There were Christmases in Great Neck, wonderful times when, in my childish eyes, my mother and dad transformed the Kensington house from an everyday, ordinary place into a magical place of colored lights, gleaming ornaments on a giant fir, the tangy scent of the tree itself filling the air with the very perfume of Christmas.

Without my mother and without Evie, Christmas had lost much of its glow, but on every holiday since she died candles were lighted in my heart for her. The carols were sung, and the tree carried in and dressed. The presents were exchanged, and the prayers said for the day that celebrates Mother and Child.

I could remember many Christmases, some with fun as well as sadness. One Christmas in our New York apartment Evie and I had a specially wonderful tree, loaded with baubles and artificial snow that glittered in the lights' shine— red, gold, blue, silver, green. That was the famous Tree That Fell on Father. Paul and Peg Stewart were helping us keep the day. In the evening, as we sat relaxed and reminiscing, the tree slowly toppled onto Dad, who was temporarily lost in a welter of branches and smashed ornaments.

We helped him up, and he stood glistening like a snowman in the debris. His eyes twinkled as he lisped in pretended outrage, "What a terrible thing to happen to a nice Jewish gentleman on Christmas Day!"

Like a lonesome child with a bag of candy, I tasted the memories slowly, making them last. There were the recent Christmases, when Evie and I were one of Hollywood's Happy Families, minglers with the "A" Group, Ed Wynn's son and attractive young wife. We had swapped presents with the big names in town, sipped their eggnog while they sipped ours, made a holiday together in spite of contract snobbery and the competitive spirit of actors on the way up and actors on the way down.

When this slow savoring of Christmas Past carried me up to the previous year, there was some glow left even there. Evie and I had already settled on a divorce, but we kept

Christmas untarnished for Ned and Tracy. We'd set up a tree and observed the old traditions of reverence—carols, Star, tree-burning on Twelfth Night.

Now here it was, Christmas of 1947, and not a light had been lit yet for me. Van had telephoned: "We want you to eat with us. The boys will be looking forward to it, and we can have a great time together."

I was thankful for the invitation. I gave Adolph the day off and set out for Evie's new home, with some extra packages for Van's new family under my arm. I had been scrupulous about Christmas shopping. Under my own tree I left gifts for everyone Evie and I regarded as our close friends. In the refrigerator I had eggnog ready for the callers I knew would drop in later in the day when I got home from eating the Johnsons' turkey and mince pie.

Walking up his driveway, I suddenly wondered whether I'd done the right thing in coming. I'd visited them dozens of times since their marriage, but the dates on the calendar had been different. This was a day that a man should spend with his own family.

Minutes after Van had opened the door for me, I knew I had made a mistake. Ned and Tracy lived in this house, not with me. They were growing used to Van as a stepfather who wanted to be a good friend. Evie was brisk and hospitable as always, but now she was Van's wife, not mine, and she was pregnant with his child. I was an intruder.

No more than an hour had passed before the feeling got too strong to resist. I was sorry about the upset I was causing, but I couldn't stay. "Please forgive me, VJ, but I can't eat with you—not this year. I've got to go. I hope you understand."

I hurried out and for that moment wanted never to go back. I went home to my empty house, where I decided I'd be better off waiting for the callers to start dropping by.

It wouldn't hurt me to miss eating Christmas dinner for once.

I put on the lights of the Christmas tree and sat in an armchair admiring it. I almost wished I'd arranged to spend the day with Dad in New York, but everything would be fine again once the doorbell started to ring, the way it had in the years before. The clock on the mantel showed 1:00 P.M.

An hour went by, and I began looking out the front windows to see if anybody was coming up the driveway. I thought a drink would help, so I poured some whisky and sipped it. I'd stay with it instead of eggnog when we had some drinks together.

I got to thinking about Dad, which wasn't the best way to spend the day, but he was part of my broken-up family, and family was a comfort I was missing badly. I could just imagine what these good people we knew in Hollywood would say when they came in: "Merry Christmas . . . how's your father?" Something like that. Then, emphasizing their great regard for him, they might add, "Boy, you'll never be half as good as your old man."

That was the way it went, and nothing to fight on this day of the year. I poured a second drink. Had I ever tried to be as good as my old man? I doubted it. I'd never worked with him, for one thing. I didn't even do the same kind of work. It would have been completely wrong to attempt it, to appear in any picture or show with Dad. They'd say, "What can the kid do? He can't be very good. His old man gets him the jobs."

It seldom did anything but harm to an actor who worked with his father. Sure, the three great Barrymores—John, Lionel, and Ethel—started with their family, but that was back in the days of family theatre, and those days were dead. Look at George M. Cohan, Jr., one of the old Great Neck gang. He was spoiled by going to work with his father.

So his big contribution to the theatre turned out to be an imitation of George M. Cohan, Sr. A miraculous imitation, certainly, but only miraculous when the two of them had been on stage together. And now who remembered George M. Cohan? The hands on the clock showed 3:00 P.M. I filled up my glass again.

In pictures, I worked with kids incapable of playing leads. They looked adequate in the finished product, because it's easy to fake in a movie and easy to make a lousy performer look better than he ever could be. But that was no good for the boy concerned. He attained no balance in his career, lacked all the groundwork. Trouble was that if I worked with a man and thought he had no talent, he realized it within thirty minutes of our meeting. I couldn't apply the old soft soap, and the old soft soap was the secret ingredient if you wanted to get ahead in this town. Some town.

If I had twenty-five per cent less talent, I thought fuzzily, I'd be better off. That much less talent and that much more *chutzpah*, which is Yiddish for gall, drive, the special brand of brass that worked so well in this industry. I'd been screaming for years that I was a good actor and they weren't using me to anybody's advantage. But nobody listened. How long could you scream about how good you were without getting sick of the sound of your own voice?

By now I had settled down to some authoritative drinking. The doorbell had not rung. Neither had the telephone. But the lights still twinkled on the tree and the packages lay heaped on the floor under its branches.

What chance did any actor have of building a reputation in good parts when he couldn't afford to pick and choose the roles he played in, when he had to consider first and foremost how to pay the rent? I'd been paying the rent for a long time now. With Ned and Tracy to provide for, I'd be paying the rent for a long time to come. So it was a squirrel's cage you worked in, getting nowhere, keeping nothing, the damn-fool son of the Perfect Fool.

I had to watch out or I'd start pitying myself. Self-pity was a drug, a lethal habit. There must be some sons who succeeded. Think about them. Think about, say, Douglas Fairbanks, Jr. There was a man who had a most difficult time and yet performed a remarkable job for himself. Nobody could have started with the odds piled higher against him. Nobody could have been in a worse position. His father was the biggest of all stars in the silents. Then his son came along and went into the same business, doing the same kind of cloak-and-dagger job, with the same name to carry like a cross. They still talked of Douglas Fairbanks, *Junior*, but he had created his own identity.

Then I knew a guy named Tyrone Power. As a newcomer to movies he was more or less my contemporary. Tyrone was a man to the manor born, the fourth generation of a line of Shakespearean actors. Yet he became an actor in spite of his father's fame. When his father died in the middle of his first movie, Ty went back to New York. He made his way as an actor before he came back to this town, and his mother went with him to the première of *Lloyd's of London*, when his career went *veroom*.

There was a man. He knew he was going into the Marines a year before he enlisted. So he ran a mile a day, worked out in the gyms, did everything to make himself a perfect specimen of health. The first day he was in uniform he got into four fights and won all four of them. This movie star was a better Marine than the average man, a better fighter, with more guts, doing a better job in the war.

He had his bad times, but he surmounted them. Anybody going into the Marines who'd been a pretty boy in movies was going to be damn near murdered before he got started. But Tyrone Power made it when the chips were down because he was a better man that most of the fellows in the services who went in with him.

I couldn't compare myself with him. I couldn't think clearly any more. I was caught in a morass of self-pity, alone, with nothing here and nothing to look forward to in love or happiness. I was drunk, and I went on drinking. Sometime in the middle of the afternoon I passed out on the floor.

At four o'clock the telephone started ringing. I was dimly aware of the noise, but I couldn't get up to answer it. Then the doorbell started to ring too. I listened from a long way off to the two sounds pealing against each other. Somebody was knocking on the door. I could hear it open, and I felt glad a visitor had arrived at last.

Cary took one look inside. I was sprawled out next to the Christmas tree, my head propped on the unopened packages. He put down the package he had brought for me and checked to see that I was only drunk, nothing worse. Then he picked up the jangling telephone.

Dad was calling from New York. "Who is this? Is anything wrong there?" I could hear Dad's voice.

"This is Cary Loftin. I'm a friend of Keenan's."

"The phone's been ringing and ringing so long I was getting worried, you know. Where is Keenan? Is he there?"

"He's fine, Mr. Wynn, just fine."

"I'd like to talk with him, please."

"He can't talk just now," Cary said. "He's taking a shower."

Dad's voice was full of suspicion. "He's drunk, isn't he? I've been thinking about him, all by himself there, and I'm positive he's been drinking."

"No, he's taking a shower, that's all. I'll ask him to give you a buzz later. You can depend on that." Cary was calming and convincing. Dad was satisfied.

"Be sure he calls, won't you?" he said. "And a merry Christmas to you." He hung up.

Cary came over to me again. "You had anything to eat yet?" I shook my head woozily. He picked up the phone again and dialed his house. "Dolores," he told his wife, "better set another plate on the table and make a place for Keenan. I'm bringing him home for Christmas dinner."

It took black coffee, the shower he had mentioned, and a change of clothes before I was ready for the trip. Then I made the call to New York; Dad and I wished each other all the good things proper to the season. With presents for Cary's family under our arms, he and I went out to his car.

That was the day I said a farewell to Hollywood in my heart. From that time on it would be a town I worked in, no more than that. Home to me would be Great Neck or the Harvey School, if you defined "home" as a place where you lived in spirit. Hollywood was never home. It was the place where you had to pay the rent and therefore had to work so the rent could be paid. If those were the conditions you had to live under, then there was no point complaining too loud or too often, and if there wasn't enough personal happiness in the situation to cover the head of a pin, then that was just your bad luck, brother.

The "A" Group had passed by my door that day, and this hurt for a while. The people I'd called friends withheld their friendship when it would have been the best gift of all for Christmas. Their names—big names in the little social game we played—were written on the labels tied with ribbon to the packages under the tree. It would take a while, too, to forget the names, if I ever cared to.

The way I felt, you could take most of the "A" Group, tie them with a big bright ribbon, and push them into the Pacific. Then you could throw their $200,000 houses in after them, not to mention the Cadillacs and the $250 suits and the swimming pools and the cuff links and the large-size, touchingly engraved silver cigarette boxes and all the other upstart junk that was presented to people who had *every-thing*.

There would be some exceptions. Bogart, for certain. Louis Calhern and the other elders of my trade, for whom I had genuine respect. Spencer Tracy, whom I'd badgered with questions as a young actor: "When will I get my chance?"

But most of the rest I had called friends, I had no time for. Friendship meant more to me than confiding how much money you really made and inviting the guy over the next time it was your turn to pour martinis. A friend was made to endure, and you'd damn near die for him if the need came. If that could be sneered at as the philosophy of a Rover Boy, then it was okay by me to go ahead and sneer, because I'd rather be a Rover Boy than a phony.

Before we reached his house, Cary glanced at me and said, "You coming out riding Sunday?"

"You bet your life I am."

I thought: Thank God for the Cary Loftins and the Hector Alexanders of this world, for all the real people who stayed with you when the going got rough.

At his house we had one more drink before we sat down to the turkey. "I give us a toast," I said. "The hell with the 'A' Group, but God bless us all."

"I'll drink to that," said Cary.

Part Four

XXI

When the sponsors lost interest in *Happy Island* only five months after the show had started, Dad entered a long stretch of doing nothing. His friends explained to each other that he "wasn't getting calls." His critics—and I had to be counted as one—saw him as an old-fashioned comic who'd reached the end of the line. For the first time in my adult life I started to feel some sympathy for him.

He hadn't had a Broadway hit since *Boys and Girls Together* closed in 1941. In Hollywood he was box-office poison. He had worn out his welcome on radio, and television was still in its early Milton Berle-Roller Derby days. Nobody wanted to hire Dad. A second marriage had ended unhappily and expensively. He fretted about so much money going out and so little coming in. He was still comfortably off, but he started to talk poor.

With nothing new in the way of theatrical success to boast about, he talked more and more about his old days as the Perfect Fool and the Fire Chief, about selling bonds in both world wars—he set some kind of record by selling 153 million dollars worth in 1945.

With no work to do, Dad started to crack up physically. He was rushed into the Harkness Pavilion for a gall bladder attack which had some complications in the shape of a nervous breakdown. He was kept in for two weeks. I was too busy at M-G-M to find time to fly East to see him.

Dad's charm continued to glow as bright as ever. I felt very little closer to him than I had in my teens, but I had to admit to some reluctant admiration for his unfailing belief in himself.

He was sure that audiences still wanted to see him and only the stupidity of producers, his lifelong enemies, kept him unemployed. He confessed he was frustrated, but he never was defeated. He echoed Grandpa Keenan, who held strong views about producers too.

"Producers are welshers," my grandfather used to say. "They don't play the game. They repudiate their contracts, deny their obligations. They're not even good gamblers. They have no idea of the power of illusion. They lack utterly a comprehension of showmanship. Given my choice between the backing of one of these with all his millions and a real showman with only a shoestring, I'd choose the shoestring, because I know that, no matter how things went, in the end the showman would fight his way through. The other fellow, smelling failure, would whimper and run."

My grandfather said that in 1923, when I was too young to understand what he was talking about. When Dad said much the same thing, I didn't listen, because it was a too familiar story.

He put together a night-club act, using pickup bits from his old Broadway hits. Any kind of work was obviously better for his morale than nothing, but he looked sad to me, in the tired old make-up, with the trunkful of props. The audiences were usually heavy with middle-aged couples who remembered him as the biggest comic in America. They brought their children to see him, and he liked that. "I'm playing now to my fifth generation of children," Dad beamed, and if you counted a generation as no more than ten years, he was almost right.

He knew he was made for something better than a warmed-over night-club act, but he wasn't sure what. He had every kind of plan for something different. He wanted, for one thing, to put an Ed Wynn revue onto film, straight and unedited, but even he had doubts whether he'd be allowed to do it. "Out in Hollywood," he said ironically, "their idea of comedy is to show some gangsters bursting open a door and finding a woman in there with half her clothes off."

He still nursed daydreams, in spite of interruptions from reality, and out of these he came up with the ambition of making a picture in which he would star as Dr. Doolittle, the nursery hero who could talk to animals. I had more chance of playing heroes myself at Metro, and my chances were plainly nil.

He would have liked to put on another Broadway production, but prices had gone up five hundred per cent since his heyday, and now he couldn't back a show with his own money. Nobody else wanted to. He wrote some sample radio shows with the thought that we'd play in them together. My enthusiasm matched the enthusiasm of producers who heard his sample records—nil.

What Dad and I had in common was new marriages. In 1946 he'd married for the third time and acquired a young stepson. On January 11, 1949, I drove to Tijuana, Mexico, with Betty Jane Butler, who had worked as a model in Los Angeles, and we were married there.

Beetsie Butler was as remote from my kind of living as anybody could be. She was the daughter of a St. Louis judge who had been wealthy until the thirties. She'd been educated in good schools, and she showed good taste in everything, except possibly in marrying me.

I had wanted this marriage to work out for us both, so the courtship was formal. I pulled in Jim and Henny Backus as chaperons for most of our outings, Jim as one of the funniest men alive and Henny to give us her blessing. I also usually tapped Jim for a dollar to tip the car-park attendant when the four of us drove out to dinner. Hard cash was always scarce with me.

After our marriage we moved into a house not far from Dad, who had bought an oversized mansion and two and a half acres as a home for his new wife and stepson. For a man who complained about the financial squeeze, this was an impressive, depressing place, with terrazzo floors, self-service elevator, and a big pool. It had been built in pre-Crash days, and it had a strong flavor of our Long Island places—old brick, ivy, privet hedges, hammocks under the trees.

Beetsie had no desire for children, which suited me because, as I saw it, the world had enough hostages of mine. I saw a lot of Ned and Tracy, who stayed weekends when Beetsie made herself scarce by going off to horse shows.

Horses were a hobby that filled her days. Our life suddenly overflowed with saddles, boots, hacking jackets, hunting pink. I bought a horse, which she stabled in a rented barn. She went out there most days after I'd driven to work.

Now I had to fit into a different Hollywood set—the horsy division, social, as distinct from the horsy division, working, of Westerns and stunt riders. "You must have chameleon blood in your veins," said Jim Backus, noting the change.

Social horsemen inhabited a tight little world of shows and hunts, tanbark rings and tack rooms. Saddles were English, stirrup leathers were short, boots were kept polished, and spurs were purely ornamental. Actors, by and large, admire horses only for betting purposes. There are exceptions, like Joe Ferrer, who do the riding-to-hounds routine, but to most of my friends horses meant cats' meat or the five-dollar window. Beetsie left them gasping.

Paul Stewart, who lived in New York and commuted to Los Angeles to make pictures, flew into town and called me soon after the wedding.

"You've got to meet Beetsie," I said. "You ought to tell her about some of the times you and I had together. All this jazz is new to her."

"Sure," Paul said. "Where'll we meet?"

She was riding in a local horse show the next Saturday, and we arranged to go there with him. He gave the scene a fast once-over: horsemen in bowlers and women in velvet caps; well-groomed animals and well-groomed crowd.

He grinned. "Where's the two-dollar window?" Horse lovers around pretended not to hear.

"Come on to the tack room and I'll pour you a drink," I said firmly.

"You mean you can't get a bet down on these nags?" We got some pitying looks from the spectators. "Pretty cheap," he said, loud and clear. "We could use a little of that five-to-one."

"Do you want a drink?"

"You mean like backstage in the dressing room?"

"Come on, and take the needle out."

He looked at the little bar Beetsie had set up in a barn and trimmed with show ribbons from her previous victories. "Booze," Paul said blandly. "This is more like it." I sucked on my pipe like a country squire and made us two stiff drinks.

Motorcycles and show horses added up to a peculiar mixture. The following Saturday, Paul came along again when I took Beetsie to watch a race on an aerodrome's runways fifty or sixty miles outside of town. In a cashmere topcoat and silk scarf she was a stand-out in the crowd.

Paul had a private question: "How's it working out with you two? You think she enjoys all this?" Bikes were pounding along the concrete. The crowd was opening up sandwich packages and cans of beer. Girls in blue jeans and boys in black leather stood hollering for their favorites.

"I guess she will, in time," I said.

Jim Backus used to say, "You're the only guy in the world who rode a bike in hunting pink." That came close enough to the truth to be funny.

We didn't visit Dad much, and he was too preoccupied to give us much thought. He was up to his ears in preparations for his new television show, as happy as he ever could be at being wanted again. He had been convinced for years that TV would sprout like Jack's beanstalk. One of the first pieces of furniture put in place in his new Brentwood house was a set he watched by the hour.

"This kind of thing," he told us, "belongs to us old-time clowns who have all the experience of vaudeville. You'll see. Television will come begging to those of us who know how to make a picture out of a joke."

It looked as though he was right. He got the invitation he'd been waiting for. He was going in as star of a revue series for the Columbia Broadcasting System. That was his first comeback.

For one season, *The Ed Wynn Show* saw him dig out every old gag and prop he'd ever devised. He found a big new audience that had never seen the Perfect Fool because they were too young to remember him or lived too far from the cities he played on the road. There was a new lease of life for the eleven-foot pole and the corn-eating typewriter. The size-thirteen boots came out of storage. He rummaged among his eight hundred hats and three hundred coats, which he'd stored with all the other relics, to choose the most bizarre getups he could lay hands on for each week's show.

"I'm back in business," he boasted. "I was sure it would happen this way."

For nine months Dad was on top of the pile again. He won the first Emmy awards as the season's star comic. A guest spot on the show was worth chasing in Hollywood. The list of names who made their television debuts with him reads like a roster of "Who's Who in TV": Lucille Ball, Desi Arnaz, Dinah Shore, Eve Arden—they were all his guests. I stuck to my rule of not appearing with him.

Then in 1950 *The Ed Wynn Show* was canceled, and he switched to NBC as one of the stars of *The Four-Star Revue*, along with Jimmy Durante, Danny Thomas, and Jack Carson. He was temporarily reprieved from losing his audience through overexposure, which is the danger that haunts every comic on a weekly series. He was also saved from physical exhaustion; doing a live show every week is one of our civilization's tortures except for the very strong or the very casual. It was a real hazard for Dad, a nagging perfectionist long past his sixtieth birthday.

Now the props and gags had to be trotted out only once every four weeks, and this helped for a while. But just as it drained his successors like Gleason and Caesar, so television killed Dad as a clown. His audience began to dwindle, but he was tied hand and foot to his format, doomed like a dinosaur because he couldn't think of changing it.

In 1953 *The Four-Star Revue* folded. Dad's option was dropped by NBC, and at sixty-seven he was out of a job again, a has-been in everybody's book. He'd never been so low as this. At the top of his early success he martyred himself over his family. When his second round of fame ended, he was martyred by the nature of this new kind of show business, and he was left washed up on the beach.

At home, his marriage was going sour in the pattern of failure his marriages fell into. He was full of aches and pains, real or imaginary, and complaints about his existence.

"I can't figure out where I am, Keenan," he kept on saying. "Everywhere I go there's this iron curtain. I talk to executives of the networks, the biggest men in television, and they all tell me: 'You're the funniest man alive, how is it you're not working?' It's very discouraging, you know."

I'd try to change the subject and leave early for home. I had some troubles of my own.

Marriage with Beetsie wasn't working out. My canter with the horsy set was coming to a standstill. She was tired of the routine, and most of the fun had gone. She couldn't fit her ways to mine, and I was set in my conflicts, like my father in his maze of misery. Adapting myself to her would have meant giving up Ned and Tracy completely to Evie and Van. I couldn't do that, so Beetsie and I decided to give up each other.

In the breakup of that marriage, it seemed to me I took one more step closer to understanding the lives of my mother and father: a marriage, I realized, could die and neither husband nor wife could be blamed.

XXII

In the middle of marriage to Beetsie, my contract with M-G-M expired after seven fat years of frustration. In pre-television days the studio contract system saved an actor from the hand-to-mouth existence that was a tradition of the theatre. Instead, he lived from one contract to another, approaching every new signing date wondering whether he ought to enlist for another stretch and worried in case he wouldn't be invited to.

The Metro bosses said, "We want you with us for seven more years. We'll start drawing up the contract now." Though, as always, I needed the money, I wasn't sure that security came above everything else, the way Dad insisted. I didn't know yet what I wanted to do with myself. But I knew the time for making up my mind was approaching fast. I didn't want to tie my hands in advance.

"Let me sign for one year," I said. They agreed to that, at a cut in salary.

More than ever, I felt I was being phony to myself. It was basically dishonest to go right on taking their money for what I considered the crummy pictures they made and the lousy parts I got. The conviction was growing stronger all the time, but I didn't have the strength of purpose to do anything about it.

M-G-M had fallen into the habit of making mediocre movies under the delusion that they were good. I had got into the rut of a professional griper. I was making pictures so horrible I couldn't stand seeing them. My friends used to go to the previews or the openings, then come back and say reassuringly, "You know, it wasn't half as lousy as you thought it was going to be." That was the best they could find to say. I usually thought the pictures I made were so bad that they could not possibly have lived up to my expectations or else every seat in the movie house would have emptied by the time the show was over.

The push I needed to break away came suddenly out of two incidents that occurred within a month of each other but ten thousand miles apart. In the first week of 1953, on the way back to the United States after a camp-show tour of Korea with Peggy King and Debbie Reynolds, I was admitted to a hospital in Tokyo with a virus attack. In a bed that seemed to float, I sweated out a murderous fever and wondered how in the name of God I had got to this point in my life.

I was feeling like death half a world away from home, except that I didn't have anything worth calling a home. I was pushing on toward my fortieth birthday, yet after two marriages I hadn't a wife to call my own, or any family apart from two sons who lived in another man's house and a father I had only begun to understand. The prospect looked so everlastingly dreary that the only way to avoid feeling sorry for myself was to do something about it as soon as I was flown State-side.

The first thing I did when that happened was try to find a steady girl.

One of my pleasures was in mixing with most kinds of people. I could swap shop talk with mechanics, pick up groceries in a supermarket, drink with the beach bums and far-out types who inhabit the canyons that run down to the ocean at Santa Monica.

That last hobby sometimes took me into a fun joint run by a fellow studio worker, Pat Dorian, where the college kids stopped by for beers in the afternoons and the traffic in the evenings went for sterner stuff. The first night I visited the place after the flight back from Tokyo I noticed a redhead that I wanted to meet. By the time I got to looking for an introduction, she had gone.

The next morning I went after Pat and asked him, "Who was the crazy-looking redhead last night?" He couldn't clearly remember the girl I meant, but he guessed: "You must mean Sharley Hudson. Santa Monica girl. Goes to the beach a lot. You want to meet her?"

"Get me her phone number, and I'll give her a call."

She gave Pat her number, and he passed it along to me. "I knew who Keenan Wynn was," Sharley said later, "but that didn't mean much to me. I figured: 'If he calls, okay; if he doesn't, I don't care.'"

It started with a blind date with the wrong girl, the way they used to play it with Jack Mulhall and Dorothy Mackail just after the talkies arrived. It developed into the kind of romance you used to see in movies twenty-five years ago, though even M-G-M had discarded that plot as too corny by the time I got to Hollywood.

I wanted the whole thing to go right, with no suspicion on the girl's part that I was another actor wolfing around for jail bait. The first night I telephoned we made some conversation, and I promised to call again. The second night I asked her to dinner and arranged to collect her at her home.

Before I rang the doorbell, her mother had the story muddled. She thought her twenty-year-old daughter had a date with Ed Wynn. "Don't you think he's a little old for you, dear?" she asked. "I used to hear him when you were a baby."

I stared and kept staring at the trim carrot-haired girl who opened the door. She took a look at me, including the beard I was wearing at the time for *All the Brothers Were Valiant,* and said, "Hi! Come on in." I continued to stare as I followed her into the living room to be introduced to her mother, sister, and eight-year-old brother. Something had gone crazy and wrong.

"Forgive me," I said, "but I've never seen you before."

Her blue eyes snapped. "What do you mean?"

"You're not the right girl. I'm sorry."

Now some Irish blood began to show. "Well, in that case, don't feel you have to take me out. Just forget it."

"Please don't misunderstand. I think you're extremely attractive——"

"Just let it go."

Everybody but the two of us thought this was funnier than *I Love Lucy.* Mrs. Hudson was shaking with laughter. I knew I was dead with this girl unless I did something impressive and theatrical. I went over to her mother. "May I have your permission to take your daughter out tomorrow night?"

Then Sharley started to giggle. I joined in. We began our life together laughing, and we've tried to keep it bright. But there were some old unforgotten things she had to hear of first. The next evening we drove out to a restaurant, and over dinner she listened while I talked about all the yesterdays. She listened closely, her eyes innocent, and I judged there'd be some part of the old days she'd always be too young to reach. We made another date for the following night.

Now that she knew something about me, I wanted to find out some of the things that made up this girl called Sharley

Hudson. I picked her up again in the Jaguar I was running, and that night I let her drive. She had an MG of her own, and she handled the Jag impressively well, manipulating its four-speed gearbox, driving like somebody who would understand my feelings about automobiles.

So the next day I put her to one more test: how would she feel about motorcycles, which were also a tremendously big part of my life? Wearing ski boots and her brother's blue jeans, she rode pillion on the Triumph. We headed for the hills. Five miles off the main roads we came to an intimidating climb on the trail.

"I can't go up that," she protested.

"Then start walking," I said, not meaning it.

"Well, in that case," she said, "when do we start?"

I was now very sure that we were two of a kind in some important respects. On our fourth date, driving over Coldwater Canyon, I said very fast, "I want to marry you. I don't know when because Beetsie and I are no more than separated as yet. But you are going to be my wife."

I sensed her smile in the darkness. "What can I say except yes? I'd be scared to say anything else when we are going this fast."

The next day, by the kind of coincidence you didn't find even in "B" pictures, was St. Valentine's Day. I had the florists' boys arriving at her house every hour. When I telephoned, she said, "Keenan, it's wonderful of you to send these thousands of flowers, but we've run out of vases, and now we're putting bouquets in milk bottles all over the house."

"What does your mother think about your getting married?"

"Right now she says the guy's crazy to spend all his money buying flowers. But she likes you very much. It'll be okay, I know, though my father's going to need some persuading."

I never did find out the name of the tall girl I'd seen at Pat Dorian's bar. I didn't ask any more. From meeting Sharley to the time we were married, we saw or talked to each other at least once every day. She didn't want to be an actress or a pillar of society, only a wife to me. She had courage and, in a strange way, the same down-to-earth sense in which I had always found peace. She was unimpressed by anything people pretended to be, only by the way they behaved. There was an extra attraction: she came from a big English-Irish family, two hundred relatives by her count, all living in California. All living—that was wonderful and important. Sharley, who had never known death in her family, thought in terms of the future, not the past.

The future nearly came to an end a week or so later. Sharley had been to a dentist to have two wisdom teeth extracted. So when I finished work, I stopped off at the florist's almost next door to M-G-M to pick up a little basket of flowers to take around to her. I put them on the front seat beside me.

On the road to her house I braked hard at a stop sign. The basket slid onto the floor. As the light changed, I bent over to pick up the flowers, one hand on the wheel and my foot pushing the gas. In the moment of straightening up, with the basket in my hand, the Jaguar sideswiped a car, which I'd failed to see, parked outside a restaurant.

My head snapped forward, my throat smashed against my own steering wheel. The whole front of the Jag was a mess. So was my face. The brittle plastic sunvisor had shattered as I struck it, and a broken piece was sticking out of my forehead an inch from my eyes.

I made it into the restaurant. I managed to get a waiter to call Sharley, then looked for the driver whose car I'd hit so we could exchange license numbers.

Sharley got a telephone call that sent her running to her

car. "Mr. Wynn has had a serious accident," the waiter ex-
aggerated, "and is asking for you." Her face was puffy from
dentistry; she wore blue jeans and not a lick of make-up when
she raced through the restaurant door, but through the blood
trickling into my eyes she looked good to me.

"You'll have to have stitches in your head," she said. "I've
got to take you to a hospital." When I tried to object, I
found I'd lost my voice. We left the Jaguar to be towed
away, and she drove me to the emergency ward at Santa
Monica.

There'd been no police call on the wreck, but a photographer hustled into the emergency room while I was in a
chair, with a doctor doing his needlework and Sharley waiting outside.

With the needle and suturing thread still dangling and
blood oozing, I jumped up. "Doctor, should he be in here?"
I croaked. The doctor was fuming: "How dare you break
in here? Get out!"

The photographer was persistent. "Whether you like it
or not, I'm going to take his picture." He aimed his camera.

"You're in the right place," I growled. "You take that picture and I'll make a hospital case out of you."

The row we were making brought Sharley in as well as
two orderlies. On the doctor's orders they got rid of the
photographer, and finally Shar and I were allowed to go.

"You mustn't let him go home alone," the doctor told her.
"Take him where there are people to keep him awake. Give
him cold drinks and, above all, don't let him fall asleep tonight. When his throat starts to swell from the bruising, he
could choke to death in his sleep."

The whole Hudson family was waiting for us. Shar's father
went shopping for a case of cold beer. They took turns in
two-hour watches sitting up—Sharley, her mother, and

father. All I could do was listen while they talked. I couldn't utter a word, but the beer tasted fine.

Somehow, I had to introduce Shar to Dad. I guessed he'd charm her from the moment they met, then probably dismiss her in his mind as just another girl. One afternoon I took her over to his house to swim. Then the three of us sat around on his lawn trying to be polite to each other. I had guessed his reactions accurately enough, but not hers. She was respectful but immune to his charm. After a strained hour or so, as we left she said, "Thank you very much, Mr. Wynn, for a wonderful time," and she went on calling him "Mr. Wynn" until long after we were married.

My own feelings toward Dad had been changing. Here was no sudden, overnight transformation of resentment into love. Only in tales told to children can the past be wiped out with a sweep of the magic wand. But little by little I was seeing my father as a man and feeling my heart warm toward him. I'd call him in the evening if he happened to be alone; meet him on the street and put an arm around him.

In this change of heart, a thousand things were involved. Perhaps the most important was something an old friend of Dad's said to me: "You know, for years after your mother died, Ed used to drive out and put flowers on her grave. And you know something else? He never told you that because he was sure you wouldn't believe him."

Sharley had a lot of catching up to do to know what kind of man she'd promised to marry. There were friends of mine to meet to fill in some background for what Jim Backus promptly christened "the memory hour." "Tell Shar about the time you and I played in *Hitch Your Wagon*, Jim." Or: "Paul, remember the day you came out to see the Gold Cup race? Tell Shar." Or: "Cary, what about that first ride you and I took together? She's never heard that story."

She came cow-trailing and rode behind me on the bike,

with the good sense not to try to change that. "You've been riding for heaven knows how many years," said this practical young woman, "and you'd probably go on riding whatever I said." She even dipped a toe into show business so we could stick to our "see you every day" promise.

I was due to leave on my last camp show. "You won't get rid of me that easily," she said. The only way she could get transportation and billeting was as a working entertainer. So she learned some patter to do comedy routines with me and with Walter Pidgeon. There was one item in the memory hour that didn't get passed on to her: Grandpa Keenan once told his second wife, Margaret, "I am going to make an actress of you for a short time. I expect you will be rotten, but it will not matter in these sketches." As a matter of fact, Sharley turned out to be somebody the GIs loved.

On our way home from the tour, six months after Beetsie and I were divorced, the chaplain on Raney Air Force Base, Puerto Rico, married Sharley and me. I prayed to God that this time it would work, and prayers were needed: the two of us had some growing up to do, Shar now twenty-one and I who was almost twice her age.

No wedding present came from Dad. He accepted her, but that was all. And to her he was still the remote "Mr. Wynn."

Half a year later, on the advice of our attorneys, we were married again, at the Little Brown Church in the Valley so there should be no doubt about our marital status in the Golden State of California. Shar was proudly and obviously pregnant.

When we first sat and talked our way to knowing each other, I'd been against the idea. "No more children at my age," I said.

"Why, that's ridiculous! Every woman wants children. I

certainly do. If that's the way you feel about it, I don't want to marry you. I'd rather call the whole thing off."

So we came right rapidly to the next question, which was when? My inclination was to wait until the marriage had settled down and established itself. "But I don't want to wait for children, Keenan. I'm young, and I'd like to start your second family right away."

She'd made up her mind about something else. "We ought to keep your two families different. I've decided to have girls, if that's okay from your point of view."

The girl I married had a rough time of it. She gained weight every day—ten, twenty, thirty, forty pounds. Even her maternity clothes only just stretched around her. Her feet were swollen up with the load they were carrying. Her obstetrician wanted her in the hospital just to rest her legs. She refused, and went on gaining.

The doctor wondered if there could be twins, and he fancied he heard two heartbeats with his stethoscope. But X rays proved he'd heard only one beat and its echo. "I've only one baby on the way," Shar reported cheerfully. "The rest is me." The scale swung around to a fifty-six-pound gain before she was admitted to the hospital for the birth.

Where she was overweight, I was underworked. In the eight months following our second marriage ceremony I had exactly one job at M-G-M. This was the sad era of decline for the Big Studio. The contract list was melting fast as some stars found their options dropped and others ran scared and resigned. The same held true for every level of studio worker. Television had landed with a bang, and all the old-line movie makers could do was complain about it.

With picture production close to a standstill, I had a lot of time on my hands to mooch around the house or mooch around bars. By Metro's standards I was one of the lucky ones who was still a desirable employee. The contract was always renewed.

"Why not sign for five years?" Benny Thau had said. "You'll soon qualify for the pension plan." Benny, one of the Big Four at M-G-M, had always been a good friend to me.

"I don't want to sign for that long; you know that."

"Aw, you'll be here all your life," he said. He meant it as a compliment, but he set me thinking more furiously than before: *What do you want to make of yourself?*

This question had grown giant-sized by the time 1955 arrived, and I was making still another picture, still the hero's best pal, still the man who got splashed when Esther Williams jumped into a swimming pool. By my count, it was the sixty-eighth movie since I'd come out from New York thirteen years ago.

The figure haunted me. Because Shar was expecting to go into the hospital any moment, the studio had eased up on its rule that barred me from driving anything while a picture was in the making. I was allowed to drive off for some location shooting in the Porsche I was running. It had to be a Porsche, and a Volkswagen for Sharley, because I had a partnership with Tom Bamford, an old motorcycle buddy of mine, in a garage that held the local Porsche and Volkswagen franchises.

I was at the wheel of the Porsche, thinking moodily about movie number sixty-eight, when another car forced me off the road. The Porsche rolled over once, lost both doors, rolled over twice more, then gave a half flip and landed on its roof. I walked away from that one with nothing worse than scraped elbows.

Back home three days later, I rented a Ford and set off in that for Vic Damone's bachelor party on the eve of his wedding to Pier Angeli. On Wilshire Boulevard a car ran into the Ford. I had to go back to the rental office and switch to a Chevrolet while the Ford was fixed.

"You'd better leave me the Chevy and take my Volks-wagen," Shar said the next morning. "Otherwise, you'll never get anybody to insure you for anything."

Outside the M-G-M barbershop, where I'd stopped for a shave, I parked the Volkswagen. A truck hit it. That made three wrecks in five days, and I blamed movie number sixty-eight, at least partly.

It took a while to screw up enough courage for what had to be done. But at last I was feeling fine. I could see the way I wanted to go—to be myself, independent as possible, to find out what I amounted to. Benny Thau had unconsciously helped to scare me with that line about "all your life." From Sharley, the crusader, I'd gathered a new kind of strength.

"Honey," I said, "I've got to make a move. I'm going to leave M-G-M."

She wasn't surprised. "A man's got to do what he thinks is best for himself."

"It may not be easy to get jobs. These are rough times in the picture business."

"So it's a gamble. I'm crazy enough to live in a tent if we have to. If you don't do it now, you never will, and then you'll be miserable the rest of your life."

"It means giving up whatever security we've managed to lay hold of."

"The heck with security. You've got to be true to yourself. Right now, you think you're cheating."

So I let my contract lapse and I walked out of M-G-M. I was out of a job for the first time in thirteen years. I had one good reason for being scared. Upstairs in our house we had a daughter, two months old.

She was born in Hollywood Presbyterian Hospital on Janu-ary 27. She and her mother had fancy outfits from Saks Fifth Avenue bought by Shar and charged to Dad, on his instruc-tions. One reason he was delighted to do it was because a new grandchild helped take his mind off his personal trouble, which always darkened his joys. In the same week our daughter was born, his third wife filed suit for an expensive divorce.

But now he qualified for something warmer than "Mr. Wynn." Shar called him "Grandpa," and he liked that. As for the baby, she'd been named long before she was born. There could be only one name for the girl Sharley was determined to bear. That, of course, was Hilda.

XXIII

There was a period of three months after I left M-G-M when I had no idea whether I could get enough work to pay my way. I couldn't find jobs at my old pay scale. Wherever I went I met with the same reaction: "Who wants him? The hero's best friend? He's never played anything else."

Nobody could remember me as anything except he-who-gets-splashed. The few good pictures I'd made were usually "B" pictures that didn't get the première treatment or reviews in the best newspapers and magazines. Suddenly income had vanished and outgo, with Hilda in the family now, had increased.

"If things really get tough," Sharley said cheerfully, "we can always put the house up for sale. It's perfectly possible to bring up a baby in an apartment. Millions of people do."

In the middle of going the rounds of the agents, making the telephone calls, doing all the hundred things an out-of-work actor has to resort to, I discovered myself thinking, *This is the way it is for Dad.* We had something else to share—job-hunting. Only for him there'd already been two solid years of it, going back to the day NBC dropped his option.

Virtually every day there'd been a producer he had to see, an idea to talk about, but nothing came of his efforts. He called on Max Gordon and J. J. Shubert. He sounded out every television, radio, and motion-picture executive he knew or could obtain an introduction to. The doors were usually open for him, walking in and coming out.

When I met him, he'd assure me, "I've got something cooking. There are still millions of people who want to see Ed Wynn." He had plans for a radio show which was to be some kind of cavalcade of show business dating back to the time he started in Philadelphia. He had a scheme for a television comeback in which he would be master of ceremonies on a series where members of the audience would try to work crazy inventions designed by himself and Rube Goldberg. He was bubbling with enthusiasm for a while about starring in a fantastic movie to be called *Wonder Kid,* in which he would play his own son.

But in fact the only work he could get was playing guest spots on other men's television shows—Red Skelton, Ed Sullivan, George Gobel—and taking his sad old night-club act to one of the Las Vegas places, where the audience applauded politely and murmured, "Isn't it wonderful after all these years?"

The disappointments affected his health. As the aches and pains started to multiply, he felt his age for the first time in his life. "Every time I pass a funeral parlor," he said wryly, "they tip their hats to me." And when the last of his divorces became final, costing him half of all he owned and twenty-five per cent of whatever he earned in future, he put his oversized house on the market and rented an apartment on Wilshire Boulevard with the thought: "I signed a three-year lease, which was optimistic, to say the least.

Moving was a melancholy experience for him. He had two rooms of the house and the double garage filled with the relics of his past. Everything had been saved, and it all needed sorting to see what was worth saving now. He'd kept the hat two-feet tall and shaped like a humming top that he wore as a stage-struck schoolboy playing amateur nights in Philadelphia. He had scrapbooks of crumbling newspaper clippings dating back to the turn of the century: "Isaiah Leopold announced yesterday that he would devote the rest of his life to theatricals. . . ."

There were photographs of my mother as a strikingly beautiful girl on tour with Grandpa Keenan; as a bride; as a young mother. There were school reports from Harvey, schoolboy letters, pictures of a spoiled brat wearing ringlets and a sailor suit. There were complete recordings of every Fire Chief show.

He had collected all the ledgers of his productions and some of the bills he had paid: for the musty costumes stored in the travel-stained leather trunks, for the scenery he ordered, for repairs to the *Seawyn* and the *Missouri Mule*. Some of the things he gave away, but most of it went back into warehouse storage.

He showed up at our house one day with a bespangled devil's costume that some forgotten chorus girl had worn in one of his Broadway shows. It was a present for Sharley. "It would be nice to wear to some masquerade party," he said. On another visit—and he'd taken to stopping off more frequently these days—he arrived with a collection of fire chief's helmets. "They're wonderful, Grandpa," said Sharley, touched by this gesture. "We'll make over the den and hang them up for decoration over the fireplace."

Every time he called, he brought something for Hilda—a doll, a soft toy, a new rattle, chosen with a grandfather's care and pride. She was the first child he'd ever had time to get to know and play with, and he treated her as if she were the only child in the world.

But he remained dissatisfied. Most of the time when he wasn't trying to track down jobs he padded restlessly in an old silk robe around his apartment, yearning to be on again.

He could never admit to himself or to me that the great Ed Wynn was living in an eclipse. He wasn't that kind of man.

I had started to live on television. The first assignment, found like many other jobs by my friend and adviser Dick Steenberg, had taken me to New York for a *United States Steel Hour* play called *The Rack*. I took Sharley along for good luck and for the sense of security she managed to instill. I hadn't worked in New York for thirteen years. I'd closed in 1942, and now it was 1955. The New York group of actors I'd worked and kicked around with had all but vanished, except for one or two old-timers like Len Doyle, who was on the show with me. The newcomers were strangers.

On the plane flying to New York, riding in a cab from Idlewild, in the city itself at first, I wasn't recognized. After sixty-eight movies, kindhearted people could only almost recognize me. "Hey!" a man would say. "Don't I know you? Wasn't I in the Army when you were?" Or else: "You from Cincinnati? You look awful familiar." Or maybe: "Sure, I spotted you right away. I seen you in pictures. You're Ken Wyman."

The U. S. Steel show was big that year, and *The Rack* won an audience of perhaps thirty million people. I figured that one performance had been watched by as many people as had seen half the motion pictures I'd ever played in. This was a completely different kind of acceptance. Overnight "Ken Wyman" turned into somebody millions of men and women could identify accurately, because they'd seen him in show after show while they sat at home. For obvious reasons, I rated this a big improvement over the movies.

Then Joe Ferrer invited me to do a movie for him. *The Great Man*, in which I was going to play a money-grabbing promoter, was a story about a sham hero. Joe also needed a character actor to handle what was essentially a one-scene role, a long monologue describing the phoniness of the "great" man.

He was temporarily stuck. Hume Cronyn, his first choice for the part, wasn't available. Burgess Meredith didn't want the job. Then Dad's agent, Kurt Frings, who was Joe's agent, too, came up with the idea that Dad could be the proprietor of a small-town radio station who saw the truth about the hero.

Joe called me: "Do you think your father could play this part?"

"Joe," I said, "it would be ridiculous to ask him. He'd never do anything like that."

"Do you think he *could* do it?"

"I don't know. With you directing him, maybe. He could submerge himself maybe."

"He can't be Ed Wynn in any way. He's got to forget about being a clown and act a part. Suppose I call him and suggest he talk it over with you?"

That was agreed, and a call soon came from Dad: "Please stop by the apartment as soon as you can. I want to ask you something, Keenan."

I didn't look forward to this, but I knew I had to go. For thirty years I'd shrugged off any advice he had to offer me. Why should he listen now? Still, I figured we'd made some progress in getting closer to each other when he would at least ask for my advice. He wouldn't admit to me or anybody else that he couldn't find jobs, but he was ready to listen to what I had so say on a subject I knew something about, which was dramatic acting.

We faced each other across his living room, crowded with furniture and mementos from his old days. "Should I do this *Great Man* part, Keenan?"

"I think it would be wonderful for you, Pop. It's not too big for you to start with. Why not try it?"

"You mean play it without my make-up and funny clothes? Destroy the character I've built up for more than fifty years?"

"You could try it." I was getting tense.

He stayed with the thought of his audiences. "It isn't fair to them to appear as the fellow next door. They expect me to make them laugh, not make them cry. What will people think of me after all these years?"

I couldn't tell him, "They don't care any more." I asked myself: *What kind of courage does it take to hurt an old man's pride? What kind of sense does it make to hand out advice he'll never accept?*

As gently as I could I said, "What can you do with the funny clothes, Pop? Nobody's buying them now. The guy with the hats belongs to another age."

He was shocked, as I knew he would be. "I've never spoken a straight line in my life. How can I start now? You don't understand, Keenan. A clown is apart from people. He isn't anybody real."

I thought I should leave before I lost my patience and we started to quarrel again. "Are you kidding, Pop?" I said. "Anyway, I still think you should do the part for Joe."

He did. "You made a lot of sense," he told me later. "I thought it was darned good advice." At first it looked as though he'd exchanged a set of old problems for a new load of trouble, but there was no limit to Joe's patience. He knew he had to deal with a man who, understandably, regarded himself as his superior in theatrical knowledge and experience. Joe was a big success in the theatre, and had been for something like fifteen years, but this was like a drop in the bucket compared with Dad's working life of half a century.

He handled the thing with real skill. He asked Dad over to his house to read the part for him. Not to audition, because Joe had earmarked my father for the part, but to run through the role together. Dad read it one way, and then Joe read it entirely differently, exaggerating the difference between his heavily dramatic interpretation and Dad's still half-comic version, so that the final result would come on target somewhere in the middle of the two readings.

Dad had to be given the feeling that he was putting the part together himself. As a dramatic actor, he had to have this sense of strength and contribution, or else he could amount to nothing in the role. They worked together for three days on the fourteen hundred words Dad had to speak.

"I can't help worrying, Keenan," he said one evening. "Imagine me after all these years coming out of the dressing room as a human being, when I've always had the protection of costumes and make-up. It's a mental upheaval, you know."

It was Joe's ambition to shoot the monologue without a break in a single can of film, which holds one thousand feet of celluloid. This meant complicated maneuvering of camera, lights, and microphones. Dad had to be word perfect for the shot to succeed.

The evening before the shot was to be taken, Joe invited him around again. He went up to Joe's bedroom and went through the scene flawlessly. Joe found himself in tears, deeply moved by the sincerity of the performance.

"My wife's downstairs with some guests," he said gently. "Will you come down and repeat what you've just done here?"

Dad bridled. "Are you serious? Are you telling me: 'Come over and bring your banjo?' I've never met these people before."

"You won't have met any of the crew on the set tomorrow either," Joe said. It took more persuasion and a stiff drink to get Dad to face the first serious audience he'd played to in the first serious role of his career.

"When I had finished," he said later, "all the women were crying. It was very encouraging." He thought he'd become

an actor in a few easy lessons. That worried me more than
anything.

The next morning I wanted to watch him without his seeing
me. When the time came for shooting, I lurked behind a flat.
I'd no last-minute word of good luck for him. For one thing,
he'd be too proud probably to accept it. For another, I was as
much afraid for myself as for Dad. I had a certain responsibility for getting him there. What came next if he failed? I
had no idea.

On Joe's signal the camera crew moved into action. Dad,
cued by Joe, began to speak, while the technicians moved
around him, silently and surely. He had complete control for
perhaps a minute, and then he faltered. It was imperceptible
except to someone who could read what was happening behind his wrinkled forehead. He had forgotten his lines. I
waited for the roof to fall in.

Joe said afterward: "I suppose it was one of the really
moving moments of my working life. You could feel yourself
cringe for the old man and feel the effort of that polished
steel brain as he reached down into his memory for the words
he'd lost. Then his real class as a performer showed. He hadn't
quite got the lines back yet, but he seized control of himself
and the situation. He ad-libbed the *sense* of his speech, and
somehow that was more moving than the words he couldn't
entirely remember. Then suddenly his memory started to
click again, and he slid back into the lines as written."

When Dad had finished some seven minutes later, the crew
cheered him. Joe ran over to him, his face wet with tears he
couldn't control. The working day wasn't over, but Joe was
more than satisfied. He kissed my father like a son. "That's
it," he smiled. "Go home now." Dad nodded his head and
wept too.

I came out of hiding, as tense and trembling as though I
were the father and he a prodigal son. We embraced. For

that moment, our sorrows were so completely forgotten that they might never have existed.

The Great Man was no more than a warm-up for the far bigger challenge he took on, unknowingly, as his next acting assignment. He suddenly told himself, "This is dramatics? Well, I can do this. It isn't so tough. What's all the fuss about?"

Word of his performance in Joe's movie had spread in Hollywood, though the picture hadn't yet been released, and Martin Manulis, producer of *Playhouse 90*, wanted him to play in *Requiem for a Heavyweight*, a ninety-minute-long live television drama.

I knew nothing of this because I'd gone to Japan to do a picture called *Joe Butterfly* for Burgess Meredith. My agent telephoned me in Tokyo to ask whether I'd do a *Playhouse 90* show. The series had only just started, but the news that Rod Serling had written *Requiem* was all I needed to know. I said yes, with no idea that Dad was in it.

The day I got back to California, I called Dad to say hello, as usual. "I've got to talk to you," he said hurriedly. "We go to rehearsal Monday."

"What do you mean?"

"Haven't you got *Requiem?* Well, I'm in it too."

I could feel my heart skip a beat. By this time I knew something about the play. Jack Palance was starred as a declining heavyweight fighter, Mountain McClintock. I was cast as his greedy manager. There was one great part left, the fighter's faithful trainer. That was going to be Dad's role.

I raved silently against his stupidity in taking it.

He would not be playing a monologue but against many different actors. Palance, for example, almost frighteningly powerful. Myself, who'd always refused to appear in anything with my father. He'd have many different scenes, changing fast in pace and emotion. I knew enough about live television by this time to be certain he hadn't a fraction of the experience necessary for an assignment where there could be no disguising of mistakes, no second tries once you were on the air.

"I don't think I'm going to do it," Dad was saying. "The part isn't big enough for me."

I skipped another heartbeat. Now I had to argue against my own convictions. "It's a fine part," I said. "I wish I had it. I'll trade with you."

He was half convinced and eager, anyway, to demonstrate to the world again that dramatics were easy. "Come over Sunday night, Keenan, and let's take a look at it," he said.

We went over the script line by line, page by page. This wasn't lowering himself, in his estimation. This was a brain surgeon consulting an eye surgeon, because their two fields of endeavor were entirely different. He could ask my advice because I'd been in my particular branch of the business longer than he had.

However they came out, I was uneasy that our appearance in the play together would carry a certain carnival flavor: Two Wynns in a Gripping Human Drama of Life in the Prize Ring; though we'd both played in *The Great Man,* we'd shared no scenes. And I was scared in case the inevitable emotional turmoil of rehearsals tore open the old wounds we had inflicted on each other which had now started so happily to heal.

Going over the script, he listened carefully to the suggestions I had to make. You can't give an actor readings at any stage of preparation or you'll stultify his interpretation. Suggestions will do a better job of highlighting the emotion of the lines.

He continued to grumble that the part was too small until the cast was brought together for the first run-through. But he went there with supreme confidence, positive that he would be brilliant. None of us was prepared for what happened. I had suspected that he couldn't possibly be more than adequate. In fact, he seemed hopeless. He could do nothing right. Few of the lines as he read them made any sense at all.

When actual rehearsals began, things deteriorated even more. Dad ambled around like a man in a dream, confusing everyone else in the cast as much as himself. With a lisp that got thicker as his confusion increased, he mangled the sense of the lines he managed to remember. Without his knowing it, an understudy was brought in, ostensibly to play a bit as a bartender but actually to step in if Dad continued to be incompetent.

Within a few days almost nobody was prepared to defend him. The director, Ralph Nelson, wanted him out. Rod Serling was more outspoken—if Dad stayed, he would insist his name as author be deleted from the credits. Something had to be done, and it looked as if it could only be my job to do it. Otherwise, Dad was going to ruin the play and shatter his own newborn reputation as an actor even before *The Great Man* was released. The only possible thing was to be frank.

I went to him and said, "You're trying to learn in a few days what it takes most men years to learn. How to speak lines, how to move around the stage, how to sustain a character. Nobody believes you can handle it, Pop. I think there's only one thing you can do to satisfy everybody and that's withdraw from the show."

He couldn't believe me. "I know I've had my difficulties," he said, "but I shall work into the part. You will see."

I felt I should not accept his answer. I telephoned Martin Manulis: "You've got to help. This man has got to be out. It will destroy him if he stays."

"Keenan, he goes on," Marty said decisively. "The show has

been advertised. He'll be fine." Then as an afterthought: "Show me a scene."

Over a lunch hour in the desolate, almost empty rehearsal hall, I joined Manulis, Ralph Nelson, and Rod Serling for Dad's trial by his peers. I played a sample scene with him. He was not good, though he was obviously improving.

Marty's mind had been made up in advance. "Look at me, I'm in tears," he said when we'd finished the scene. "It was beautiful."

I wanted to hit him. "You know he's brutal, though he's trying," I whispered to Marty.

"He's going to be in it," he said, and that was that. He had to have Dad on that program. For a producer the "draw" is important, the advertised attraction that commands the big audience. It was Marty's determination that kept Dad in *Requiem* in spite of everything.

"You've got to make him good," Marty said. "You've got five days left. Get with it."

Concentrated effort was required from everybody. Dad still had trouble with his lisp, his hands, his walk, with his grasp of the character of the old trainer. Neither he nor I slept much during those few days. We met every night with a special coach who'd been assigned to him. There was one contribution only someone close to Dad could make and that was to dig back into his life for clues to make him feel the emotional truth of his part. We did that, line by line through the script.

For example, he had a line, "Good-by, Mountain," which was his farewell to his fighter. On those two words Dad's voice wavered up and down like a roller coaster.

I interrupted him. "Pop, how old would you say Earl Benham is?"

"He's seventy. Why are you asking me now?"

"Well, then, think of Mountain as though he were Earl.

Say good-by to him as if you were never going to see him again." It worked. Dad could say the line now to bring a lump to your throat.

From rehearsal hall, *Requiem* went on to the floor for two days' rehearsal with cameras before air day. On the second day of constant run-through, Dad had forgotten his lines, his moves, everything. At dress rehearsal on air day, he blew every other line. He was doing remarkably well in the sessions at home with the coach and me, but here on the floor he would fluff, then stare up at the camera and say, "I'm sorry." And it was only a matter of hours before we were on, coast to coast.

I couldn't think straight. The tension was greater than I'd ever known before in my life as an actor. I tried to give him a final pep talk. "Pop, don't look up; you can't do that. Forget the microphones. Don't stare at the cameras. You mustn't apologize for anything." Do this, don't do that—it seemed utterly, desperately hopeless.

Jack Palance is a kind and gentle man. He did everything possible to help, though no actor can help another once the other guy starts *his* lines; all you can do is listen and pray. At one point, Jack had to hit Dad, hard, in a scene. He is an ex-fighter and conscious of his physical strength.

"Mr. Wynn," he said softly, "I just may hit you in this scene, but I'm going to be careful, you can be sure."

Dad smiled faintly. "I couldn't think of any way I'd rather go," he said.

Now Dad and I were in the dressing room we shared, and we were on in a few minutes. I was a wreck, hands dripping with sweat, head spinning with anxiety. "If you miss a line," I was gabbling, "I'll say it, Jack'll say it, somebody. Just get through this play and don't worry. Okay?"

"Okay," he said, with a kind of calm.

Now we were doing the long walk (*music under*), Dad

and I carrying Jack down a long corridor to the dressing room. We were on. We carried Jack into the dressing room and lifted him onto a table. Dad had the first line. I waited for it, getting frantic. He was silent. I was all set to ad-lib when he spoke. A perfect line. I thought: *We've got it made. Isn't this great? Isn't this fine?*

Then there was another complete silence. I thought: *Who talks now, for God's sake?* I had forgotten it was my turn. I blew five lines in a row. Jack covered up for me, Dad had to ad-lib for me, before we got back on the track. Then, before the first scene was over on that Thursday night of *Requiem*, you could feel the play take off and fly.

We had only one problem, and that was inevitable. In one scene I had to glare at Dad and sneer at him, "You've got the biggest nose in the business, wise guy."

This was supremely difficult. You couldn't disassociate yourself from the relationship completely and be exclusively an actor when the man you confronted was your father.

Dad was startled for an instant and stepped out of his character to be Ed Wynn again for just three words. "Oh, my goodness!" he gasped. Then he went straight back into a great performance.

At eleven o'clock that night, Ed Wynn had re-established himself. A whole new career had opened up for him. We both wanted to get home in a hurry to see the filmed repeats that would be televised for West Coast audiences. I went up to our dressing room in the side of one wall of the three-story-high CBS studio to pick up our clothes.

I wanted to be alone for a moment, too, to think about what might happen to us now Dad was the great Ed Wynn again.

When I came down, he was surrounded by a crowd of perhaps two hundred people. He'd been somebody that nobody wanted for days, weeks, years. Now he was himself again, the center of attraction for the crew, other actors, technical staff, network men, advertising agency, and sponsors' representatives, who were pouring in their applause while he nodded and bowed and beamed.

I stood on the outskirts of the crowd, holding our coats, and calling, "Hey, Pop, we ought to get going! Hey, Pop!" But I couldn't get through to him. Suddenly I realized I was Ed Wynn's son all over again.

XXIV

Dad was suddenly up to his ears in work again and, understandably, tremendously pleased with himself. Like an old fire horse hearing the brass trumpets toot, he was off and running to answer the television and motion-picture offers that kept his telephone ringing. He galloped between Hollywood and New York to make movies like *Marjorie Morningstar* and *The Diary of Anne Frank*, to appear in TV plays like *The Great American Hoax* and *Protégé* and in his series as John Beamer, which was labeled *The Ed Wynn Show*. He even uncrated one of his inventions again, the combination of bicycle and keyboard he called his pianocycle, and shipped it to New York, hoping to ride it as a guest of Perry Como.

"You'd think I was somebody they never heard of, the way the phone goes on ringing," he told reporters and magazine writers who found that the Perfect Fool was making good copy for them again. "Either there are a lot of lousy actors around or I'm really wonderful." Of course, he thought he was really wonderful. He was back in his old form in those interviews.

"I've become a sort of Elvis Presley for the middle-aged," he said to one magazine. "Only the people who swoon over me have difficulty getting up again." He always had the knack for ad-libbing that kind of good, sharp-edged gag.

Hollywood had become largely a television city, and that helped Dad as well as me. One of the happy things that happened in television was that type-casting died, and with that, the stage-trained actor came into his own.

The purely movie-trained actor doesn't always fare too well in a world of television, though a stage-trained performer is geared to it. You do twenty-six minutes of finished TV film, a normal half-hour show, in three days of shooting. In a movie studio that would take three weeks. The movie-trained actor is used to doing two lines, then "Cut!" He isn't used to rehearsing, but to playing himself all the time. In television this method doesn't work. You can see some of the big names from movies try it, and they damage their reputations in the attempt.

When that happens, they swear they'll never expose themselves again to the trials of TV. That's like an ostrich sticking his head in the sand. Some stars are wealthy enough not to care. But I think a lot of them would be well advised to start worrying and looking for jobs in some other line of business if they need rent and eating money.

They delude themselves with the belief that movies are going to "spring back." I anticipate that movies will survive—just as vaudeville survived—but in a very different form from the one we were all accustomed to. In vaudeville today there are a few highly specialized acts that play Las Vegas, Florida, and New York. I think in the future there'll be a few movies too, and they'll be good ones.

If you live on movies today, you either have to be one of the Big Twelve, like Kirk Douglas or Bill Holden, or else a strange new breed of performer which is now in fashion: the almost-a-star who keeps getting parts without being able to play them; not every time, anyway.

The men who make pictures get crushes on actors and persuade themselves that the only way they can earn profits is by employing those actors. The front offices believe that with those actors in the cast the pictures must automatically be money-makers. The producers and the bankers behind them point to a movie like *The Bridge on the River Kwai,* which grossed eighteen million dollars in 1958, as proof that Bill Holden, who was one of its stars, can guarantee the profits. They gloss over the fact that *The Key,* in which he also starred, brought in only $2,200,000.

John Wayne is one of the big draws in movies, no doubt about it. Yet *The Barbarian and the Geisha,* his most important picture in 1958, earned only $2,500,000, and something called *The Legion of the Lost* grossed $300,000 less than that. I may be wrong, because I'm not in the business end of it, but it strikes me that, quite apart from having a star to play in your picture, you'd better have a good movie too.

In older days, you played a movie part—he-who-gets-splashed or anything else—and the studio kept you playing similar roles, afraid that audiences wouldn't accept you in anything else. In television I've played everything—heroes, heavies, cops, tycoons—and audiences apparently are intrigued by that. Until Dad worked in TV—as an actor, not a comic—they liked my work before they knew who I was. Then along came *Requiem,* the two of us were working in the same business again, and the old distasteful problem reared up once more, the problem of my identity. Dad regarded the darkest period of his decline as the days when, with some pity for himself as well as humor, he used to say he was "the father of Keenan Wynn, the actor." I know he found it as humiliating as I did when I was called "Ed Wynn, Jr.," which I never had been.

But I was getting pulled down to the dismal level of being "Ed Wynn's son" again, after I'd been congratulating myself that this unhappy state of affairs had ended years ago. And today, at forty-three, I am still Ed Wynn's son, although not as strongly as before.

There has been a powerful purpose for this book in my mind: I set out to throw some light on the problems of sons and their fathers. Clearly, this is a universal conflict dating back to Cain and Abel. Every boy born of woman spends part of his life overshadowed by his father. If the father helps his son achieve independence, makes sure he walks on his own when he's old enough, then this span of difficult years can be short. If the boy is "the boss's son," there are extra handicaps—he has to deal with flattery as a child—but in the average, healthy family this, too, can be handled easily.

The sons of famous men have special problems all their own. The parent's fame casts bigger shadows. The son may have a real fight on his hands to survive as an individual. I am an example of this.

I am a working actor making good money. I haven't yet achieved the position I seek, but I think I might in time. Three years ago I had reached a point of individuality where, with Dad forcibly retired, only people in my business readily appreciated the relationship between Ed and Keenan Wynn. Now his reputation is reborn, which gives me a rare, peculiar feeling, impossible to resent; I am thrilled that he is working, delighted that he has had a return to enormous popularity. And when I start to feel uncomfortable about it again, I hold onto the love I have lately found for him.

The big fight is with myself, to pull away from the state of self-pity which I remember from the past as a morass in which a man can enslime himself. I smell it in the presence of some of my contemporaries who are in similar situations, the children of the famous. I have great admiration for those of them who keep out of this mud.

There is a man who was christened Creighton Chaney, known nowadays as Lon Chaney, Jr., because Universal-

International Pictures Corporation wanted it that way. He and I have worked together, and he's an effective actor. One day I asked him, "Did you ever have difficulty being Lon Chaney's son?"

He didn't reply for a moment, then said, "Let me just tell you this. I am a grandfather with five grandchildren. I have been an actor twenty years longer than my father was. I've been making pictures almost thirty years since he died. I'm middle-aged now, and they still call me Lon Chaney, Jr. Does that answer your question?"

Any son who works alongside his father runs into additional discouragement; he's suspected of getting the assignment because "Daddy wants to give me a job." I have never regretted staying away from Dad in every show until two years ago. It was the best thing for both of us, just as he was perfectly right when I started out in the theatre and he got me an Equity card, a box of make-up, and my first job in summer stock. His attitude was: "Now let's see what happens." It was one of the few lessons in independence I had from him.

I am sure every working actor whose parent is a star has the same problem of submerged identity—John Drew Barrymore; Eddie Foy; Mickey Rooney; John Wayne's son, Pat; Joel McCrea's son, Jody; Jason Robards; James MacArthur, son of Helen Hayes; all of them.

One member of the Crosby clan who faced the problem in spades and beat it is Bob Crosby. Though he looks and sounds like his brother, he has just kept plugging away and building a good reputation for himself. I did a guest shot on his morning TV show one day. Naturally, he came out with the fateful question, "What's it like being Ed Wynn's son?"

There was only one answer: "What's it like being Gary Crosby's uncle?"

The children of actors suffer only a mild form of the frustration. I shudder to think what it must cost a man who obviously has great interior strength, Major John Eisenhower. What a miserable time he must have faced! This is a man who cannot be given all the promotion he deserves because to do so would look like playing favorites. I feel certain that all Sir Winston Churchill's children have a difficult time, like all the sons and grandsons of old Henry Ford and all the line of John D. Rockefeller up to and including Nelson. It must be that way.

A young man named Lance Reventlow is an amiable guy who does what he knows best, which is developing and racing sports cars. Morons criticize him as a crazy kid, but he's no idiot. He has expert mechanics, body men, and drivers working with him, and he's achieving results from the time and money he has invested. But at the Riverside race track outside of Los Angeles the other day, I heard an employee snarl at him, "What are you doing here, millionaire? You want to buy your way in?"

I dread the son-and-father situation building up around Ned who has ambitions to be an actor too. He is going to find people saying, "How's your grandfather?" and "How's your father?" and, "How's your stepfather, Van Johnson?" It'll take five minutes before he hears the question which must be most important to him, which is, "How are *you*?"

But Ned never stifled in the atmosphere of big money that Dad enjoyed when I was my son's age. Financially, neither Van nor I has approached Dad's kind of spending money, not in these days when taxes skin you. Ned didn't live like a boy behind a wall of gold brick taller than his head. Unlike me, he also has an embarrassment of parents. Evie, Van, and I remain good friends, and now Sharley is part of the equation. The four of us rode out recently to put Ned on a plane at Los Angeles International Airport to take him East for enrollment at the University of Pennsylvania. Evie and I stood together at the gate saying an almost tearful farewell to our first-born, while Sharley and Van stood by smiling sympathetically.

Because the Johnsons and the Wynns are friends, another day is noted in the memory hour. I'd been taking care of Ned and Tracy for a weekend, and on Monday morning I took them back to the Johnson's house. As we let ourselves in as usual, we heard sounds of a slight domestic spat; nothing sensational, just a man-and-wife clash of opinions. Then Van came into the den, flushed with the argument. He saw us and fired a question that proved personal histories are easily forgotten: "How'd you like to be married to a girl like that?"

Cary is a frequent caller at our house. We still ride on Sunday mornings with the Triumphs roped in a trailer hitched to the rear bumper. He grins, though, now and asks, "Do I need a stop watch or a calendar to time you today?"

I have become an "oh-oh" rider: "Oh-oh, trail's getting rocky; better slow down" and: "Oh-oh, there's a guy going to pass me; guess I should let him." It wasn't like this before, when I was trying to prove something to myself: "I can do this. I can lick the lot of them. I'm not just a rich man's spoiled brat."

I was ignorant and young, which gave me courage of a very limited brand. Now I've got to the point where I've done most of the proving of myself to myself that I have to do. I still go out on the hills like a boy, but riding is a cathartic, to ease the tension when it builds inside. There may be three hundred starters in a hare-and-hounds ride, and I'll be lucky to finish, but I get back home a nicer guy than when I left.

XXV

My father has become the epitome of every old actor. Everything he does makes the same silent point: "Look at me. I'm on. Isn't it wonderful?"

It's hard to sympathize with his compulsion to work—making a weekly television series, for instance. He doesn't drive himself this way for money; he has more than enough for his needs. Nor for power, since he has never felt that particular hunger. Only because he cannot live without public attention.

He had a finger on the pulse of his audiences for more than fifty years, and he made a great commercial success by providing the kind of laughter they looked for. As a clown with no personal happiness, he lived for applause and by it. He hasn't changed in that respect. Applause is still the pay-off.

And we still quarrel—though the old fury has gone—about such mundane things as the price of the new kitchen cabinets Sharley wanted to install.

Dad is her faithful escort when I'm away from home on a job. He takes her to dinner at Chasen's or some other fashionable hangout, and he's delighted when heads turn and other diners whisper, "There's Ed Wynn with a young redhead."

So to cut short speculation, he introduces her very explicitly: "This is Keenan's wife; this is Sharley."

When he calls at the house, his charm remains so dazzling he's probably welcomed by the two-year-old parakeet that so far has never uttered a word and the goldfish which has survived a bubble bath whipped up by young Hilda in its bowl. Dad arrives with presents under his arm and lollipops in his pocket. He has two granddaughters now; Sharley stuck to her resolve by giving birth to Edwyna, called Winnie, in 1957.

Dad was the first to reach the hospital that day. He had been telephoning Shar almost every hour to ask about her progress. During the last weeks if she happened to be out when he phoned, he went into a spin. When her time came she rang him, and he was waiting for us at the reception desk when we got there at seven o'clock one morning. As Shar came out of the delivery room, Dad was on one side and I was on the other. As a name, Edwyna pleased him as much as Hilda.

Sharley has looked after another generation's needs too. She came across the grave of Grandpa and Grandma Kate Keenan in the Hollywood Cemetery. Its neglect horrified her. She had the grass cut and the weeds pulled. Now the headstone has been cleaned and flowers planted. When his turn comes, that is where Dad has said he would like to be.

He used to insist in his prime, "If an actor wants to stay successful, he has to marry the public and stay married." But the years softened the harshness of that ambition. He has thought more and more of the girl he married. "One of the great thrills of my life," he said one day, "was your mother."

One day I shall bring her from the Gate of Heaven to the family grave. I know that is what Dad will want.

I have learned that every man has two kinds of growing up to do. One determines how the world sees him; the other, how he sees himself. These are the differences between body and soul. By all outward signs I matured young, put on some muscle, looked like a man while I thought as a boy. In the other, more important way—the ability to see myself as an entity—I have only just grown up.

Out of this self-discovery, I sympathize with my father as a fellow man shaped by his triumphs and defeats and anxieties, as all men are, instead of regarding him as a father image wrapped in guilts. And this new-found relationship with him is only part of the prize of self-knowledge. Belatedly I can put a punctuation mark to the battle inside between Catholic and Jew.

Behind the bar in the paneled den of our house hangs a painted sign. It was a present from my cousin, Keenan Sloan. He is my mother's sister's son; we are like brothers. It consists of a quotation from William Blake, and it says:

> The only Man that e're I knew
> Who did not make me almost spew
> Was Fuseli: He was both Turk and Jew—
> And so, dear Christian Friends, how do you do?

I am partial to the words, and I have the right to smile at the problem because I am Fuseli in person. Our own family lived through a tragedy of misunderstanding which built such pain in my mother's heart that in the end it destroyed her. But that was a long, long time ago. I can appreciate finally that on the subject of race relations the Cohens and the Kellys are every bit as significant and truer to our times than the *Merchant of Venice*.

By my mother's standards, I have to regard myself as a bad Catholic. In Los Angeles years go by without my attending Mass, which is contrary to the duty of men who believe as I do. Yet, in a sense, I may be a better Catholic now than I was in more dutiful, less understanding days.

In the course of learning to appreciate something about Dad and the things that made him, I stumbled on some basic principles of Christianity. That the human race is one race, not many races. That all men are created by God and loved by Him. That the Son of God didn't die for any single creed or segment of mankind but for all humanity. I could have accepted none of that, except with meaningless lip service, in my "better" days.

To the surprise of many friends, I remain a Catholic. That's what it says on my passport, on my overseas ID tags, and within myself. It would be unthinkable to change. And on visits to New York, I sometimes go to St. Patrick's to pray, to remember my mother and all the sad days.

One morning recently I turned off Fifth Avenue into the Cathedral under the two Gothic spires. I counted the steps— first four, then three—the way I used to when I crossed the avenue to go to Mass with my mother from the apartment on West Fiftieth Street.

Pushing through the embossed doors, I went down a side aisle, one of the hundred bits of humanity gathered there to pray. I walked past the stone figures of St. Brigid and St. Bernard, St. John the Baptist de La Salle, St. Augustine, and the mosaic of the Holy Face of Our Lord; past the flickering candles.

I turned by the white-lighted statues of the Family and skirted the confessional boxes and the waiting line outside them. In the Lady Chapel behind the altar, I sat down and found, as usual, a kind of peace.

It used to be that I prayed for only one parent; now I can pray for two. I used to feel sometimes that prayers were better directed toward the Virgin than toward God, because she was the mother. But such heresy is part of the past and only a memory.

I doubt whether there could have been any short cuts on the road to understanding. I believe in free will and therefore in guilt and evil, so the psychoanalyst's couch has no attraction for me. But in St. Patrick's, in the dim light that comes through the stained glass, I have been helped to understanding.

I realize there are deep-down affinities between Catholic and Jew, that Catholicism is built on Jewish principles of Godliness and love. In that sense, we are all descendants of Abraham. As a Pope once said, spiritually we are all Semites. The mother of the Son of God was a Jewish maiden.

My mother was a Catholic and my father a Jew. Out of that difference a world of antagonisms was born that swamped the three of us. Of course it need never have been that way. Given enough real faith, charity of heart, and love, all that was inevitable about the outcome was that I had to be a crossbred mutt.

Now in my family there is a new generation of mutts, two boys and two girls. I doubt whether anything could be healthier for them.

As for myself, I am still extremely conscious of being my father's son, but nowadays I am proud of it. And I am enormously proud of him for achieving all he does at seventy-two. I'd like to be half as fortunate when I'm that age.

I am deeply aware of something he put in words just the other day: "To be loved by your fellow man, Keenan, is one of God's greatest gifts." For my part, it took a long time to discover what love means. But between Dad and me there has developed a great love, a man-to-man devotion. I realize that in our mixed-up family life it was his love that made it possible for me to grow up. There were years when I deserted him. But he never deserted me.

If there is any lesson in my story, it is this: A lot of kids, like me, will always run away from their homes and the hearts of their families. But some kids, like me, are lucky because there's a light left burning in a window for them.

Dad kept a light burning for me—Ed Wynn's son.

Postscript

A new weekly TV series called *The Troubleshooters* was looking for a sponsor not long ago. The lead in the show is a television discovery named Keenan Wynn. A phone call came from Dick Steenberg, my partner and business brain of *The Troubleshooters*. He was delighted for us both: "Texaco's very much interested. Isn't that something? Same company your father worked for as the Fire Chief."

I had a kind of vision of judgment. The siren wail. Dad in a fireman's hat to handle the commercials and introduce, "My son, Keenan." The whole show dominated by his opening and sign-off.

It was too much. I said nothing at all.

Dick is a sympathetic soul. He could guess what I was thinking. He unsold fast—and found us another sponsor.